AN ACCOUNT

OF THE

MUSICAL PERFORMANCES

IN

WESTMINSTER-ABBEY

Da Capo Press Music Reprint Series

MUSIC EDITOR
BEA FRIEDLAND
Ph.D., City University of New York

AN ACCOUNT

OF THE

MUSICAL PERFORMANCES

IN

WESTMINSTER-ABBEY

BY

CHARLES BURNEY

New Introduction by
PETER KIVY

DA CAPO PRESS · NEW YORK · 1979

Library of Congress Cataloging in Publication Data

Burney, Charles, 1726-1814.
    An account of the musical performances in Westminster-
Abbey.

    (Da Capo Press music reprint series)
    Reprint of the 1785 ed. printed for the benefit of
the Musical Fund, London.
    Original t.p. reads: An account of the musical
performances in the Westminster-Abbey and the Pantheon,
May 26th, 27th, 29th; and June the 3d, and 5th, 1784.
In commemoration of Handel.
    1. Händel, Georg Friedrich, 1685-1759. I. Title.
[ML410.H13B9 1979]   780'.92'4   78-31784
ISBN 0-306-79524-8

Introduction copyright ©1979 by Peter Kivy

82-119
Published by Da Capo Press, Inc.
A Subsidiary of Plenum Publishing Corporation
227 West 17th Street, New York, N.Y. 10011

INTRODUCTION

I. HALLELUJAH HANDEL

IT is clear that a good many of our modern institutions and customs had their inception in the eighteenth century. This appears to be true of *musical* institutions and customs as well. And those who recall that the first public concerts on record probably took place in eighteenth-century London will not be surprised to learn that that rather questionable but nonetheless firmly entrenched musical rite, the "music festival," also seems to be able to trace its lineage back to that time, and that place. For if the great Handel Commemoration of 1784 was not the first of the breed, it certainly was the first in the modern mold. Indeed, every modern inconvenience of Salzburg, Edinburgh, or Tanglewood, was already palpably present in Westminster Abbey, on Wednesday, May 26, 1784, the first day of that "ur-festival," when, Charles Burney tells us, "such a croud of ladies and gentlemen were assembled together as became very formidable and terrific to each other, particularly the female part of the expectants; for

V

some of these being in full dress, and every instant more incommoded and alarmed, by the violence of those who pressed forward, in order to get near the door, screamed; others fainted; and
all were dismayed and apprehensive of fatal consequences: as
many of the most violent among the gentlemen, threatened to
break open the doors..." (*Commemoration*, p. 25). (Even the
English in stays were not so staid, after all). Nor will the contemporary habitué of music festivals be unfamiliar with the conditions that prevailed on the second day of the Handel Commemoration, in the Pantheon, where "The extreme heat of the weather,
augmented by the animal heat of more than sixteen hundred
people, closely wedged together, must have considerably diminished the delight which the lovers of Music expected to receive
from this night's exhibition: when the body suffers, the mind is
very difficult to be pleased" (ibid., p. 45). Judging by the behavior
of these "lovers of Music" at the previous performance, the
phrase "animal heat" seems not ill-chosen.

The *Account of the Musical Performances in Westminster-
Abbey, and the Pantheon, May 26th, 27th, 29th; and June the 3d,
and 5th, 1784,* was ably, and eloquently given by Charles Burney,
the "official historian," in the volume before you; and there seems
little use in telling the story again in an introductory essay. Suffice
it to say, the Commemoration was intended to celebrate the centennial of Handel's birth, and the twenty-fifth anniversary of his
death (1759), both of which, very conveniently, came in 1784—
only, it must be noted, because the English had their dates mixed
up. The error was promulgated by John Mainwaring, Handel's
first English biographer,[1] and eternalized in marble, in Roubilac's

---

[1] [John Mainwaring], *Memoirs of the Life of the Late George Frederic Handel*
(London, 1760).

well-known monument in the Abbey. Actually Handel was born in 1685, making 1785 the centennial of his birth—but, inconveniently, the twenty-sixth year after his death. Burney's account begins, as the times dictated, with a dedication to the royal patron, King George III, written for Burney by his friend, Dr. Johnson. And Percy A. Scholes, in his biography of Burney, opines that "This really masterly little composition must have been one of Johnson's last literary tasks, if not his very last one, before he died."[2]

The volume which Burney produced in commemoration of the Commemoration is many things. It is an historical document of great value, providing information about the development of musical taste and practice in the late eighteenth century. It is, of course, a lively eyewitness account of a great musical and "sociological" event. The Sketch of the Life of Handel which it contains is one of the primary sources for later biographers of the composer. And whatever the historical inaccuracies caused by the limited documents at Burney's disposal, the character of Handel which emerges, built up both of Burney's own personal observations of the great man, and conversations with those who had known him, has the ring of truth about it, and presents to us a figure admirable in virtues, human and delightful in foibles: a kind of musical Dr. Johnson, with great sallies of wit, often censorious, but seldom cruel or undeserved; something of a heroic figure, bouncing back from adversity, steady to his artistic standards, honest and square-dealing in financial matters at a time when it must have been very easy to be lax. But above all else—and this, I think, requires some spelling out—Burney's *Account* is a mile-

---

[2] Percy A. Scholes, *The Great Dr. Burney: His Life—His Works—His Family and His Friends* (Westport, Conn.: Greenwood Press, 1971), vol. II, p. 72.

stone in the history of music criticism: therefore, an important document in the history of aesthetic thought. This is the aspect of the work that, in my view, has not been fully appreciated, and which I would like to probe in these introductory remarks.

II. MUSIC AS ART

What makes criticism possible? The answer to this Kantian-sounding question (or, rather, part of the answer) is "Art." As a consequence, what makes musical criticism possible is the art of music.

Now it has become clear, due mainly to some recent scholarship of Paul O. Kristeller's, that what he calls "the modern system of the arts" came into being in the early part of the eighteenth century.[3] That means: the arts as we think of them, literature, painting, sculpture, dance, music—the so called "fine arts"—were not always of a piece: did not always comprise that "system." More to the present point, before the eighteenth century, however music was thought of in the West, it was not thought of as "art": whatever trade Byrd and Purcell were seen as plying by their contemporaries, it was not the trade of Shakespeare and Milton. Perhaps music was thought of as "science," or "craft," or "entertainment" (or all three at once); but whatever "art" was thought to be, music was not thought to be *it*.

I am not claiming, of course, that music was not an art before the eighteenth century. I am claiming that it was not *seen as* an art until then. And when I say that music criticism is made possible

---

[3] Paul O. Kristeller, "The Modern System of the Arts," *Journal of the History of Ideas,* Part I, XII (1951); Part II, XIII (1952).

(in part) by the art of music, I mean to suggest not only that music as art is a necessary condition, but the realization of music as art as well. What made the music criticism of Burney's *Account* possible was the acceptance, in the eighteenth century, of music into the Pantheon of the arts; the taking up of music into what Kristeller called "the modern system of the arts."

It is no mere coincidence that Burney was, at once, the first "modern" historian of music and the first "modern" music critic. For in the same process by which music came to be seen as an art, music gained a "past." Burney begins his great *General History of Music* with the observation that "The feeble beginnings of whatever afterwards becomes great or eminent, are interesting to mankind."[4] Music became "great or eminent" when it became "art" in mankind's eyes; and when it became "art," its "feeble beginnings" then became "interesting to mankind." Of course, crafts and entertainments have their "feeble beginnings" as well. But to have a past is to have "feeble beginnings" worthy of mankind's interest. Music gained that status by achieving "art-hood."

To become an art, to gain a past, to become great or eminent, to gain mankind's interest: in a word, to become a complex, problematic object and, in so doing, to demand an accounting, a "critique," an explanation: that is the road I am suggesting was traveled in the process of bringing into being music criticism in general, and the music criticism of Burney in particular. But to fully understand the rather tentative, uncertain form that this criticism took, we must understand the theoretical context into which it was born. I have suggested that the eighteenth century was the scene of many aesthetic births; that many of our artistic

---

[4] Charles Burney, *A General History of Music,* ed. Frank Mercer (New York: Dover, 1957), vol. I, p. 11.

customs and institutions had their beginnings in the century of Enlightenment. Among them is one most relevant to the present undertaking. For it is generally agreed that aesthetics and the philosophy of art, as a separate specialized branch of philosophical knowledge, came into being in England, in the opening years of the eighteenth century. At the vital center of this newly established discipline was what might be called "the question of criticism," and what the eighteenth century generally referred to as the problem of "the standard of taste." To that question, as the Enlightenment formulated it, we must now turn our attention, as propaedeutic to the reading of Burney's criticism.

III. THE CRITIC'S DILEMMA

The identification of artistic appreciation with the "taste" of the palate is so venerable—it recedes back into antiquity—that it is hard to see it any longer as a metaphor. It seems no less literal to us to talk about "taste" for painting or music than "taste" for wine or cheese. Yet there is a tension here, lurking just below the surface of discourse. For whereas we are quite willing to allow that tastes in foods vary, are "subjective," lack any standard of correctness, we by no means behave as if the same is true of taste in art, about which we dispute, and pass "critical" judgment. And herein lies the dilemma of criticism. If artistic "taste" is "taste" indeed, then there should no more be disputes about art, or critical judgments, than there should be disputes about cheese, or wine-criticism. If it is not, wherein lies the canon of judgment; and wherefore has "taste" been seen as so natural a description of artistic appreciation?

Two eighteenth-century philosophers of genius posed this dilemma, and attempted its resolution: Hume, informally, in his elegant essay, "Of the Standard of Taste" (1757), and Kant, in the more formal argument of the *Critique of Judgment* (1790). Hume, being closer to home, and in the proper time-frame, will serve to throw the issue into proper relief. Burney is likely to have known his essay.[5]

It is commonly held, Hume points out, that "Beauty is no quality in things themselves: it exists merely in the mind which contemplates them; and each mind perceives a different beauty." From which it seems to follow that "every individual ought to acquiesce in his own sentiment, without pretending to regulate those of others."[6] But in the face of this "axiom" of the relativity of taste and beauty, Hume continues, "there is certainly a species of common sense, which opposes it." For, he concludes, "Whoever would assert an equality of genius and elegance between Ogilby and Milton, or Bunyan and Addison, would be thought to defend no less an extravagance, than if he had maintained a molehill to be as high as Teneriffe, or a pond as extensive as the ocean."[7] This, then, is the dilemma of criticism, as Hume lays it out. He provides a powerful (if not acceptable) resolution in "Of the Standard of Taste." But it is no part of my present purpose to go into that here.[8] It suffices for us to realize that Burney's music criticism—and music criticism in general—entered the scene at a

---

[5] As a matter of fact, Burney met Hume while they were both in Paris.

[6] David Hume, "Of the Standard of Taste," *The Philosophical Works of David Hume* (Boston: Little, Brown, 1854), vol. III, p. 252.

[7] Ibid.

[8] For my own view of Hume's position, and its defects, see: "Hume's Standard of Taste: Breaking the Circle," *British Journal of Aesthetics*, VII (1967); and, "A Logic of Taste—the First Fifty Years," *Aesthetics: A Critical Anthology*, ed. George Dickie and Richard Sclafani (New York: St. Martin's Press, 1977).

moment when the very foundations, and possibility of criticism itself were very much in doubt, and in need of philosophical justification.

That Burney's practical criticism suffered from this critical dilemma will readily be seen when we come to examine some examples of it in this volume. That his own *idea* of criticism was impaled on its horns becomes immediately apparent from the "Essay on Musical Criticism" with which he prefaces Book III of the *General History of Music*. Burney begins:

> As music may be defined the art of pleasing by the succession and com-
> bination of agreeable sounds, every hearer has a right to give way to
> his feelings, and be pleased or dissatisfied without knowledge, experi-
> ence, or the fiat of critics; but then he has certainly no right to insist on
> others being pleased or dissatisfied in the same degree. I can very readily
> forgive the man who admires a different Music from that which pleases
> me, provided he does not extend his hatred or contempt of my favour-
> ite Music to myself, and imagine that on the exclusive admiration of
> any one style of Music, and a close adherence to it, all wisdom, taste,
> and virtue depend.[9]

Clearly, this is as forthright a statement as one could wish of Hume's "axiom" of the relativity of taste and its consequences. Music is the art of pleasing with sounds. Different people are pleased by different sounds. Therefore, there is no "standard" of musical taste beyond the ability of music to please, and no critical rule whereby divergent tastes can be rationally brought into conformity. There are different musical tastes, but, apparently, no "better" or "worse"; and neither knowledge nor criticism has any admonitory force.

But, as Hume says, against the "common sense" of aesthetic

---

[9] *A General History of Music,* vol. II, p. 7.

relativism, another species of "common sense" reacts. And this is no less true where the aesthetic relativism is musical. For not only is Burney not steady to his text in his criticism, he is not steady to it even in this statement of critical principles. Thus it is not very long after Burney the relativist has hoisted his colors that Burney the absolutist has hauled them down. Indeed, as soon as the real business of criticism gets talked about, and its "first elements" laid bare, it becomes quite obvious that Burney's principles are not consistent with his opening remarks. For it soon becomes apparent that Burney the critic is far from taking his own advice seriously, to refrain from legislating good taste and sound judgment. So, for example, Charles Avison, who Burney characterizes "the first, and almost the only writer" to attempt musical criticism in England, is taken to task on the grounds that "his judgment was warped by many prejudices," as "He exalted Rameau and Geminiani at the expense of Handel, and was a declared foe to modern German symphonies."[10] But, one is forced to wonder, by what yardstick is Avison judged to be warped by many prejudices? Why should he not exalt Rameau and Geminiani over Handel, if Rameau and Geminiani please him more? For has not Burney himself declared that music is simply the art of pleasing with sound, and no man's pleasure inferior to another's?

Or, again, Burney remarks, "Of a good shake, a sweet tone, and neat execution, almost every hearer can judge; but whether the Music is good or bad...science and experience only can determine."[11] Yet we were told, at the outset, that "every hearer has a right to give way to his feelings, and be pleased or dissatisfied *without knowledge, experience, or the fiat of critics*" (my italics).

[10] Ibid.
[11] Ibid., vol. II, p. 10.

Surely these two pronouncements do not jibe. For the first suggests all of those things about artistic judgment and appreciation that are summed up in *de gustibus non est disputandum,* while the second, on the contrary, suggests that there is good music as well as bad, and bad judges as well as good.

Now my purpose here is not to take cheap philosophical shots at someone who, after all, had no pretensions to philosophy. It is no discredit to Burney that he failed to deal adequately with a dilemma that two of the master thinkers of the eighteenth century struggled with in vain. My point in bringing out this contradiction in Burney's thought is to provide a means of understanding what might otherwise seem puzzling in his criticism of Handel. For it is because Burney flourished as a critic when the "dilemma of criticism" was particularly pernicious, and because he lacked a method by which to draw its fangs, that Burney's criticism of Handel took on the character that it did. And to that criticism we must now, finally, turn our attention.

IV. BURNEY AS CRITIC

I cannot, without being overly prolix, go into the numerous ways in which Burney's criticism of Handel reflects the "critic's dilemma" I have spoken of above. But I think I can, very briefly, illustrate the kind of thing I have in mind by teasing out one persistent idea that pervades Burney's critical thought in the present volume.

In his evaluation of Handel's music, it is fair to say that Burney is almost obsessed with the passage of time from its composition to the Commemoration of 1784. And I can demonstrate this obsession only by the piling up of examples.

The Dettingen Te Deum: "'*Thou sittest at the right hand of God,*' &c. is expressed in a strain that is remarkably pleasing, and which, in spite of forty years, still retains all the bloom and freshness of novelty..." (*Commemoration*, p. 29).

Overture in Saul: "an Overture, which neither age, nor fashion, can deform" (ibid., p. 32).

The Dead March in Saul: "This most happy and affecting movement, which has retained its favour near half a century..." (ibid., p. 32).

The Funeral Anthem: "The beauties of this strain [*"kindness, meekness, and comfort were in her tongue"*] are of every age and country; no change of fashion can efface them, or prevent their being felt by persons of sensibility" (ibid., p.34).

Orlando: "But, so changed is the style of Dramatic Music, since HANDEL'S was produced, that almost all his songs seem *scientific*" (ibid., p. 49).

Ezio: "This Air [*Vi fida lo sposo*], which is in a style peculiar to HANDEL, and the period in which he flourished, has, perhaps, been robbed a little of its beauty and grace, by time..." (ibid., p. 59).

Ezio: "And though the life of a musical composition is in general much shorter than the life of a man, yet this [*Nasce al bosco in rozza cuna*] bears its age so well, that instead of fifty-two years old, it seems in all the vigour and bloom of youth" (ibid., p. 65).

Rodelinda: "and so far is the whole composition [*Io t'abbraccio*] from discovering its age, that it seems of a kind which must be immortal, or at least an evergreen; which, however times and seasons vary, remains fresh and blooming as long as it exists" (ibid., p. 66).

Anthem, My heart is indibting of a good matter: "The third

movement, '*Upon thy right hand,*' &c. is as graceful in melody as
rich in harmony; and as new as if composed yesterday, except in
one favourite passage with HANDEL and his times, which being
now a little *passé*, is perhaps, too often repeated for modern ears"
(ibid., p. 70).

Two things are repeatedly expressed in these passages: *surprise*
that Handel's compositions have managed to survive the ravages
of time; and, less often, but significantly, the opinion that the
lapse of time *has* rendered some passage or composition old-
fashioned and musically unacceptable to modern ears. And when
one realizes that the period of time in question is, at the very
most, a mere fifty years, the praise, as well as the blame, seem
puzzling and unfounded. Why are we puzzled, and why in the
first instance was Burney surprised, and in the second censorious?

Why *we* are surprised, of course, is that we are used to the idea
of there being enduring musical masterpieces; and not merely
masterpieces enduring fifty years, but five hundred years and
more. And because Burney, clearly, is not at all at home with this
idea, although he does not entirely reject it either, survival of
musical "masterworks" through time puzzles him, and musical
"fashion" plays more of a role in his critical judgments than it
would do in ours.

But *why* was Burney so uneasy with the notion that the music
of the past, even of the recent past, could still be heard, appreciated, enjoyed by modern ears? Partly, of course, it is because
music had so recently achieved "art-hood," that it was difficult for
Burney to think of it always in those terms; and "art-hood" con-
fers principles, and engenders enduring masterworks. Partly too,
however (and the point is not unrelated to the preceding), it is, I
would suggest, just because Burney was impaled on the horns of

the "critic's dilemma." True, he believed that there were firm principles on which the quality of music could be judged. And if the music of the past, even the distant past, stood up to these principles, why should it not be appreciated and enjoyed, as were Homer and Virgil? Yet he half believed, as well, that music is merely the art of pleasing with sounds; and what pleased our fathers and grandfathers is unlikely to please us, for they had their "fashions," while we have ours. After all, we are not pleased with their manner of dress, nor they with ours. "So changeable is taste in Music," Burney writes in the *History*,[12]

> and so transient the favour of any particular style, that its history is like that of a ploughed field: such a year it produced wheat, such a year barley, peas or clover; and such a year it lay fallow. But none of its productions remain, except, perhaps a small part of last year's crop, and the corn or weeds that now cover its surface.

If this indeed was Burney's view of music, small wonder he sometimes expressed surprise over a composition, even of Handel's, sounding well after fifty years, or, at times, showed himself overly sensitive to the ravages of musical "fashion." *Was* it his view? Well, it was and it wasn't—that is the critic's dilemma.

V. HALLELUJAH BURNEY

If these remarks have helped the reader to understand the tentative, ambivalent nature of Burney's musical criticism, they may perhaps have also conveyed a negative impression of Burney as critic. Such was not my intention at all. Quite to the contrary, my

[12] Ibid., vol. II, p. 380.

admiration for Burney's critical judgment is boundless. He almost always backed the right horse, and remained remarkably
open to new musical ideas all of his life. A champion of Handel,
and of J. S. Bach, although he rated Handel stronger in organ
fugue (*Life*, p. 41), in later years, an enthusiast for Haydn's instrumental music and Mozart's compositions for the voice: few
critics can boast such a record of correct evaluations. No doubt,
his Handel is not ours—nor, for that matter, is Johnson's Shakespeare. But if a comparison is wanted, I am tempted to say that
what Dr. Johnson did for Shakespeare's reputation in the eighteenth century, Dr. Burney, in a smaller way no doubt, did for
Handel's. And if we cannot accept their "revisionist" attitudes,
nurtured on the eighteenth-century idea of progress in the arts, we
can at least acknowledge our enormous debt to their pioneering
efforts in the modern art of criticism.

PETER KIVY
Rutgers University
New Brunswick, New Jersey
January, 1979

Publish'd January 8th 1785.

AN

ACCOUNT

OF THE

MUSICAL PERFORMANCES

IN

WESTMINSTER-ABBEY,

AND THE

PANTHEON,

May 26th, 27th, 29th; and June the 3d, and 5th, 1784.

IN

COMMEMORATION

OF

HANDEL.

By CHARLES BURNEY, Muf. D. F. R. S.

————— All
The multitude of Angels, with a fhout
Loud as from numbers without number, fweet
As from blefs'd voices, uttering joy, heav'n rung
With jubilee, and loud Hofannas fill'd
Th' eternal regions.   MILT. PARAD. LOST, Book III.

LONDON,
Printed for the Benefit of the MUSICAL FUND; and Sold by T. PAYNE and
Son, at the Meufe-Gate; and G. ROBINSON, Pater-nofter-Row.
MDCCLXXXV.

TO THE

KING.

GReatneſs of mind is never more wil-
lingly acknowledged, nor more
ſincerely reverenced, than when it deſcends into the regions of general life, and
by countenancing common purſuits, or par-
taking common amuſements, ſhews that it
borrows nothing from diſtance or for-
mality.

By the notice which Your Majeſty has
been pleaſed to beſtow upon the celebration

of

DEDICATION.

of HANDEL's memory, You have condefcended to add Your voice to public praife, and give Your fanction to mufical emulation.

The delight which Mufic affords feems to be one of the firft attainments of rational nature ; wherever there is humanity, there is modulated found. The mind fet free from the refiftlefs tyranny of painful want, employs its firft leifure upon fome favage melody. Thus in thofe lands of unprovided wretchednefs, which Your Majefty's encouragement of naval inveftigation has brought lately to the knowledge of the polifhed world, though all things elfe were wanted, every nation had its Mufic ; an art of which the rudiments accompany the commencements, and the refinements adorn the completion of civility, in which the inhabitants of the earth feek their firft refuge from evil, and,

DEDICATION.

and, perhaps, may find at laſt the moſt elegant of their pleaſures.

But that this pleaſure may be truly elegant, ſcience and nature muſt aſſiſt each other; a quick ſenſibility of Melody and Harmony, is not always originally beſtowed, and thoſe who are born with this ſuſceptibility of modulated ſounds, are often ignorant of its principles, and muſt therefore be in a great degree delighted by chance; but when Your Majeſty is pleaſed to be preſent at Muſical performances, the artiſts may congratulate themſelves upon the attention of a judge in whom all requiſites concur, who hears them not merely with inſtinctive emotion, but with rational approbation, and whoſe praiſe of HANDEL is not the effuſion of credulity, but the emanation of Science.

How

DEDICATION.

How near, or how diftant, the time may be, when the art of combining founds fhall be brought to its higheft perfection by the natives of Great Britain, this is not the place to enquire; but the efforts produced in other parts of knowledge by Your Majefty's favour, give hopes that Mufic may make quick advances now it is recommended by the attention, and dignified by the patronage of our Sovereign.

I am,

With the moft profound Humility,

Your MAJESTY's moft dutiful

And devoted Subject and Servant,

CHARLES BURNEY.

C O N T E N T S.

Defcription of the PLATES, and Directions for placing them.

PLATE I.

FRONTISPIECE. *The* MEDAL *ftruck on occafion of the Commemoration of* HANDEL, *and worn by their Majefties and the Directors, on the Days of Performance.*   To face the Title.

PL. II.

View of HANDEL's MONUMENT *in Weftminfter-Abbey, with the additional* TABLET, *recording his Commemoration.*
                     To face the 1ft page of HANDEL's Life.

PL. III.

Ticket of Admiffion to the Firft Performance; which being originally fixed for the 21ft *of April, to commemorate the Day of* HANDEL's *Funeral, reprefents a* SARCOPHAGUS, *with a Medallion of the great Mufician over it.*
                     To face the Title of the Firft Day's Performance, p. 23

PL. IV.

Ticket of Admiffion to the Second Performance. HANDEL *compofing facred Mufic; the Genius of Harmony crowning him, and a Seraph wafting his Name to Heaven.*
                     To face the Title of the Second Day's Performance, p. 43.

PL. V.

Ticket of Admiffion to the Third Performance. BRITANNIA *pointing to a Py-ramid, on which the Name of* HANDEL *is engraved; a Genius offering the Firft-fruits of a Sacrifice to his Memory; and on the Back-ground, a per-fpective View of Weftminfter-Abbey.*
                     To face the Title of the Third Day's Performance, p. 71

PL. VI.

View of the GALLERY *prepared for the Reception of their Majefties, the Royal Family, Directors, Archbifhops and Bifhops, Dean and Chapter of Weftminfter, Heads of the Law, and others of the principal Perfonages in the Kingdom, at the Commemoration of* HANDEL *in Weftminfter-Abbey.*
                     To face the Title of the Fourth Day's Performance, p. 91

PL. VII.

View of the ORCHESTRA *and Performers in Weftminfter-Abbey, during the Commemoration of* HANDEL.
                     To face the Title of the Fifth Day's Performance, p. 109.

P R E F A C E.

A Public and national tribute of gratitude to deceafed mortals, whofe labours and talents have benefitted, or innocently amufed, mankind, has, at all times, been one of the earlieft marks of civilization in every country emerged from ignorance and barbarifm. And there feems no more rational folution of the myfteries of ancient Greek mythology, than to imagine that men, whofe virtue and abilities furpaffed the common ftandard of human excellence, had excited that degree of veneration in pofterior times, which gave rife to their deification and apotheofis.

Such a gigantic idea of commemoration as the prefent, for the completion of which it was neceffary that

a

fo

fo many minds fhould be concentred, muft have been long foftering ere it took a practicable form, and was matured into reality. But from the conception of this plan to its full growth, there was fuch a concurrence of favourable circumftances as the records of no art or fcience can parallel : the Royal Patronage with which it was honoured ; the high rank, unanimity, and active zeal of the directors ; the leifure, as well as ardour and fkill of the conductor ; the difinterefted docility of individuals ; and liberal contributions of the public ; all confpired to render this event memorable, and worthy of a place, not only in the annals of Mufic, but of mankind.

And indeed it was hardly poffible for a Mufical Hiftorian not to imagine that an enterprize honoured with the patronage and prefence of their Majefties ; planned and perfonally directed by noblemen and gentlemen of the firft rank ; attended by the moft numerous and polite audience that was ever affembled on a fimilar occafion, in any country ; among whom, not only the King, Queen, Royal Family, nobility, and great officers of ftate appeared, but the archbifhops, bifhops, and other dignified clergy, with the heads of the law,

would

would form an æra in Mufic, as honourable to the art and to national gratitude, as to the great artift himfelf who has given occafion to the Feftival.

HANDEL, whofe genius and abilities have lately been fo nobly commemorated, though not a native of England, fpent the greateft part of his life in the fervice of its in-habitants: improving our tafte, delighting us in the church, the theatre, and the chamber; and introduc-ing among us fo many fpecies of mufical excellence, that, during more than half a century, while fentiment, not fafhion, guided our applaufe, we neither wanted nor wifhed for any other ftandard. He arrived among us at a barbarous period for almoft every kind of mufic, except that of the church. But, befides his oratorio chorufes, which are fo well intitled to immortality, his organ-pieces, and manner of playing, are ftill fuch mo-dels of perfection as no mafter in Europe has furpaffed; and his operas were compofed in a ftyle fo new and ex-cellent, that no Mufic has fince, with all its refine-ments of melody and fymmetry of air, in performance, had fuch effects on the audience.

Indeed his works were fo long the models of perfec-tion in this country, that they may be faid to have formed our national tafte. For though many in the capital have been partial, of late years, to the compofitions of Italy, Germany, and France; yet the nation at large has rather tolerated than adopted thefe novelties.

The Englifh, a manly, military race, were inftantly captivated by the grave, bold, and nervous ftyle of Handel, which is congenial with their manners and fentiments. And though the productions of men of great genius and abilities have, fince his time, had a tranfient fhare of attention and favour; yet, whenever any of the works of Handel are revived by a performer of fuperior talents, they are always heard with a degree of general fatisfaction and delight, which other compofitions feldom obtain. Indeed, the exquifite manner in which his productions are executed at the concert eftablifhed for the prefervation and performance of old mafters, ftimulates a defire in all who hear them to have a more general acquaintance with his works. And it was, perhaps, at the late performance in Weftminfter Abbey, that the compofitions of this great mafter were firft fupplied with a band, capable of difplaying all the wonderful powers of his harmony.

Pope,

Pope, more than forty years ago, imagining that his band was more numerous than modern times had ever feen or heard before, contented himfelf with calling him *Centimanus*, where he fays :

Strong in new arms, lo! Giant HANDEL ftands,
Like bold Briareus with his *hundred hands*.

But if our great bard had furvived the late Commemoration, when the productions of Handel employed more than five hundred voices and inftruments, he would, perhaps, have loft a pun, a fimile, and a *bon mot*, for want of a claffical allufion to lean on.

Notwithftanding the frequent complaints that are made of the corruption of Mufic, of public caprice, and private innovation, there is, perhaps, no country in Europe, where the productions of old mafters are more effectually preferved from oblivion, than in England: for, amidft the love of novelty and rapid revolutions of fafhion, in common with other countries, our cathedrals continue to perform the fervices and full anthems of the 16th and 17th centuries, by Tye, Tallis, Bird, Morley, Gibbons, Humphrey, Blow, and Purcell; as well as thofe produced at the beginning of the prefent

fent century, by Wife, Clarke, Crofts, and others, whofe grave and learned compofitions have contributed to keep harmony, and the ancient choral ftyle, from corruption and decay. The Crown and Anchor Concert, efta-blifhed in 1710, for the prefervation of old mafters of every country, has long endeavoured to check innova-tion; and the annual performances at St. Paul's, for the benefit of the Sons of the Clergy; the Madrigal Society, as well as the Catch-Club, and Concert of Ancient Mufic, are all more peculiarly favourable to the works of the illuftrious dead, than thofe of living can-didates for fame.

But the moft honourable eulogium that can be be-ftowed on the power of Mufic is, that whenever the human heart is wifhed to expand in charity and bene-ficence, its aid is more frequently called in, than that of any other art or advocate: as the delight it affords in exchange for fuperfluous wealth, is not only the moft exquifite which the wit of man can fupply, but the moft innocent that a well-governed ftate can allow.

Indeed Handel's Church-Mufic has been kept alive, and has fupported life in thoufands, by its performance for charitable purpofes: as at St. Paul's for the Sons of

the

the Clergy; at the Triennial Meetings of the Three Choirs of Worcester, Hereford, and Gloucester; at the two Univerfities of Oxford and Cambridge; at the Benefit Concerts for decayed Muficians and their Families; at the Foundling-Hofpital; at St. Margaret's Church for the Weftminfter Infirmary; and for Hofpitals and Infirmaries in general, throughout the kingdom, which have long been indebted to the art of Mufic, and to Handel's Works in particular, for their fupport.

This will not only account for the zeal of individuals in propagating his fame, but alacrity of the nation at large, in fupporting an enterprize calculated to do honour to the memory of fo great an artift, and extenfive a benefactor.

From all the information with which my mufical reading and inquiries have furnifhed me, it feems not too much to fay, that the muficians affembled on this occafion exceeded in abilities, as well as number, thofe of every band that has been collected in modern times: as may be reafonably inferred from the following chronological lift of the moft remarkable mufical mufters upon record.

At

At an interview between Francis I. king of France, and Pope Leo X. in 1515, at Bologna in Italy, the muficians and fingers of the French king and the Roman pontiff meeting together, formed the moft numerous band which had ever been incorporated in thofe times. The number, however, is not mentioned; but as the chapel and court eftablifhment of thofe princes could never, when united, form a body of muficians fufficiently confiderable to be put in competition with that lately affembled, the number may ftill remain indefinite, without leaving the leaft doubt of its fuperiority.

On the ceffation of the plague at Rome, in the early part of the laft century, a mafs compofed by Benevoli, for fix choirs, of four parts each, was performed in St. Peter's church, of which he was maeftro di capella; and the fingers, amounting to *more than two hundred*, were arranged in different circles of the dome: the fixth choir occupying the fummit of the cupola. On both thefe occafions no inftruments feem to have been employed, but the organ.

We

We are told in Bonnet's *Hiſt. de la Muſique (a)*, that the *Te Deum*, which Lulli had compoſed for the recovery of Lewis XIV. in 1686, was afterwards performed at Paris, on the recovery of his eldeſt ſon, Monſeigneur, by *three hundred muſicians.*

In the year 1723, moſt of the great muſicians of Europe were aſſembled together in the city of Prague, by order of the emperor Charles VI. to celebrate the feſtival of his being crowned king of Bohemia. Hiſtory, ſays Quantz (the late celebrated performer on the German flute, and maſter of the preſent king of Pruſſia), does not furniſh a more glorious event for muſic, than this ſolemnity; nor a ſimilar inſtance of ſo great a number of eminent profeſſors, of any one art, being collected together. Upon this occaſion, there was an opera performed in the open air, by *a hundred voices*, and *two hundred inſtruments (b).*

A ſolemn ſervice was performed at the funeral of Rameau, 1767, at the church of the Oratory, in Paris, by all the muſicians of the king's band, and by thoſe of

(a) Tom. II. p. 93.
(b) *Herrn Johann Joachim Quantzens Lebenſlauf, von ihm ſelbſt entworfen.* Publiſhed by Marpurg at Berlin, 1754. See likewiſe *Muſical Tour*, vol. ii. p. 177.

b   the

the Royal Academy of Mufic, united. On this occafion, we are told *(a)*, that many pieces from Rameau's beft productions were felected, which drew tears from feveral that were prefent, by the excellence of the mufic, and the melancholy occafion on which it was performed.

At *Santa Chiara*, in Naples, about the fame time, according to Signor Corri, who was then in that city ftudying under the famous Porpora, near *three hundred muficians* were employed at the laft confecration of a nun of great diftinction.

And at the public funeral of Jomelli, in the fame city, **1774**, a like number was affembled together, in order to pay their laft duty to that great mafter; and thefe not only performed *gratis*, but contributed to the neceffary expences of this folemn fervice *(b)*.

At many other *gran funzioni* and feftivals in Rome, Venice, and other parts of Italy, a congrefs of *two or three hundred muficians* is not, perhaps, very uncommon; but from the time that the prefent fyftem of harmony was invented, to this period, no well-authen-

(a) *Effai fur la Muf.* tom. III. p. 465. *di Saverio Mattei.* In Napoli, 1774.
(b) *Saggio di Poefie Latine ed Italiane*

ticated

ticated inftance, I believe, could be produced, of *five hundred* performers, vocal and inftrumental, being confolidated into one body, and giving fuch indifputable proofs of talents and difcipline, as on the late occafion.

Indeed the fortunate arrival of Madame Mara in this country, while the manner of celebrating the intended feftival was in contemplation, eafed the directors and conductor of much anxiety and difficulty, as to the diftribution of the Songs. There were, at this time, but few great fingers in London who ftood high in the favour of the public; and thofe were either inacceffible, or apprehenfive that a fingle voice, of whatever volume, would be inaudible, in fuch an immenfe building as Weftminfter-Abbey. The voluntary offer therefore of this admirable finger to perform at each exhibition, and the liberty granted by the managers of the Pantheon, to whom fhe was exclufively engaged, gave birth to hopes from fingle fongs, which were greatly furpaffed, in effect, on the day of performance. Indeed, the moft fanguine promoters of this enterprize, muft at firft have imagined, that the chief difference and fuperiority of thefe performances to all others,

would

would have arifen from the aggregate of founds produced by fo immenfe a band, in the chorufes.   But the
effects were not rendered more new, grand, and furprifing, by the united force of the whole, than fweet,
diftinct, and audible, by the fingle efforts of individuals.   The knowledge, experience, and abilities of
the two alternate leaders of this Mufical Legion, Meff.
Hay and Cramer, were never more manifeft, nor were
their orders ever more implicitly obeyed, than on this
great and trying occafion.

Indeed, the effects of this amazing band, not only
overfet all the predictions of ignorance and farcafm,
but the conjectures of theory and experience.   By fome
it was predicted, that an orcheftra fo numerous could
never be *in tune*; but even *tuning*, to fo noble an organ, was, for once, grand, and productive of pleafing
fenfations.   By fome it was thought that, from their
number and diftance, they would never play *in time*;
which, however, they did moft accurately, and without
the meafure being beat in the ufual clumfy manner.   By
others it was expected that the band would be fo *loud*,
that whoever heard this performance, would never hear
again; however, the found of thefe multiplied tones
arrived

arrived as mild and benign at the ears of the audience, as they could from the feeble efforts of a few violins, in a common concert-room. And, laftly, that from the immenfe fize of the building, no *fingle voice* had the leaft chance of being heard by thofe who had places remote from the orcheftra ; but, luckily, this was fo far from being true, that not a vocal breathing, how- ever feeble by nature, or foftened by art, was inaudible in any part of the immenfe fpace through which it dif- fufed itfelf in all directions.

All thefe difficulties, real and imaginary, were hap- pily obviated by Mr. Commiffioner Bates, the CON- DUCTOR of this great enterprize ; for this gentleman, who had fo long made the various works of fo great and fertile a genius his particular ftudy, felected the pieces, collected, collated, and corrected the books ; and, with a diligence and zeal, which nothing but enthufiafm could infpire, after the idea was fuggefted, totally devoted every moment of his leifure to its ad- vancement and completion.

There have been commentators who have dedicated their whole lives to the ftudy of one author: Homer, Ariftotle, and Shakfpeare, have had votaries of this

kind

kind; and when admiration and zeal are moderated and tempered by rectitude of judgment, those who, during a long series of years, have chiefly pointed their attention to a particular style of musical composition, must be best acquainted with its beauties, and able to direct others how to execute it with energy and precision.

No musical *amateur* had perhaps ever such experience in these matters, or such frequent opportunities of combining and disposing a numerous band to the best advantage, as Mr. Bates; who, while he was pursuing the study of literature and science at King's-College, Cambridge, had the reputation not only of being the best gentleman-performer on the harpsichord and organ of that time, but had the chief direction of the concerts and choral performances in that university; as he had afterwards at Hinchinbroke, where the earl of Sandwich frequently regaled his neighbours and friends with Oratorios, executed with the utmost precision, by performers of the first class. After the establishment of that most respectable institution, the Concert of Ancient Music, in 1776, of which Mr. Bates digested the plan, he was long the sole conductor duĉtor of the performances at thefe meetings, fo juftly celebrated, not only for accuracy and precifion, but for the new effects produced from fuch old and venerable productions of great mafters of harmony, as would otherwife have been buried in oblivion, or fwept away from public notice by the rage for novelty, and tide of fafhion.

However my mind may be impreffed with a reverence for HANDEL, by an early and long acquaintance with his perfon and works, yet, as it amounts not to bigotry, or the preclufion of all refpect or admiration of excellence in others, wherever I can find it, my narrative will be lefs likely to excite fufpicions of improbability, or hyperbole, in fuch readers as were not fo fortunate as to participate of the furprize and rapture of all that were prefent at thefe magnificent performances, and are able to judge of the reality of the fenfations defcribed.

As fuch uncommon attention has lately been beftowed on the *works* of HANDEL, it feems natural to imagine, that the fame public which has interefted itfelf fo deeply in their performance, will be curious about every thing that concerns the *perfon* of fo renowned

nowned a compofer. I fhall therefore prefix to the following account, a *Sketch of his Life*, drawn from fuch narrations as have been publifhed in England and Germany, as well as from the recollection of what paffed within my own memory and knowledge. And though I referve the critical examination of the entire works of HANDEL for the laft volume of my Hiftory, yet, as indifcriminate praife is little better than cenfure, I fhall fpecify fuch beauties of compofition and effect as I felt moft forcibly in attending the performance of each day, and for which, by a careful perufal of the fcore, I have been fince enabled to affign reafons.

After fo long a Preface to fo fhort a book, I fhall add nothing more, in apology for my narrative, than that I was ftimulated to the drawing it up, thus haftily, by the extreme fatisfaction I felt in finding that the late COMMEMORATION was not only an undertaking of fuch magnitude as to merit the patronage of an enlightened public; but that the public, by its liberal fupport and profound attention, manifefted itfelf to be worthy of the undertaking.

SKETCH

Pl. II.

E.F.Burney delin.   I.M.Delattre sculp.

View of HANDEL'S Monument in Westminster Abbey.

Published January 14th 1785.

S K E T C H

OF THE

L I F E

OF

H A N D E L.

IT is by such minute degrees that men arrive at that point of
eminence which interests the public, and awakens general curiofity, that the beginnings of greatnefs pafs unobferved, till they
can no longer be diftinctly feen through the blaze of meridian
brightnefs. Thus the early events of an illuftrious character are
generally as obfcure and fabulous, as the firft years of an ancient
and powerful empire. For Biographers, notwithftanding the
title they affume, feldom draw from the life ; nor, till an illuftrious perfonage has been fome time deceafed, do enquiry and con-
jecture begin to bufy themfelves in tracing incidents, defcribing fi-
tuations, and delineating characters. And hence, by procraftination,
the whole becomes little better than a mere *fancy-piece.*

B

If

If it were poffible, however, to know, in detail, the youthful exploits of an Alexander, or a Cæfar; the firft poetical effufions of a Homer, or a Virgil; the dawnings of reafon in a Newton, or a Locke; or the primary fermentations and expanfions of genius in a HANDEL, they would afford great gratification to human curio-fity, which delights in feeing by what minute gradations, or gi-gantic ftrides, men gifted with uncommon powers, begin their journey to the Temple of Fame.

The *Memoirs of the Life of* HANDEL, publifhed in 1760, the year after his deceafe, though written with zeal and candour, are neither fufficiently ample nor accurate to enable us to afcertain with precifion the places of his refidence, dates of his productions, or events of his early years, previous to his firft arrival in Eng-land, in 1710, at the age of Twenty-fix.

It is however generally agreed, that the great mufician, GEORGE FREDERICK HANDEL, was born at Halle, in the Duchy of Magdebourg, and Circle of Lower Saxony, the 24th of February, 1684; that his father was an eminent furgeon and phyfician of the fame place, and upwards of fixty years of age when this fon, the iffue of a fecond marriage, was born; and that, in his early childhood, he difcovered fuch a paffion for Mufic as could not be fubdued by the commands of his father, who intended him for the profeffion of the law.

He had made a confiderable progrefs in this art, by ftealth, before he was allowed a mafter; but at feven years old, his father finding it impoffible to fix his attention to any thing but Mufic, for which he feemed to have been endowed by nature with very uncommon propenfities and faculties, he placed him under Za-chau, organift of the cathedral church of Halle; a man of con-
                                                                    fiderable

fiderable abilities in his profeffion, and proud of his pupil. By the time he was nine years old, our young Mufician was not only able to officiate on the organ for his mafter, but began to ftudy compofition; and at this early period of his life he is faid to have compofed a Service, or, as it is called in Germany, a *fpiritual Cantata*, every week, for voices and inftruments, during three years fucceffively. The late Mr. Weideman was in poffeffion of a fet of Sonatas, in three parts, which HANDEL compofed when he was only ten years old *(a)*.

He feems to have continued to ftudy under his firft mafter Zachau, in his native city, till the year 1698; when, being arrived at the age of fourteen, he was carried to Berlin, where operas were in a very flourifhing ftate, at the court of the Elector of Brandenburg, afterwards King of Pruffia, who had then in his fervice not only many fingers of eminence from Italy, but Bononcini and Attilio, to compofe. HANDEL is faid to have diftinguifhed himfelf in this city as a wonderful performer, for his early years, and to have given birth to fuch expectations of his future greatnefs, that his Electoral Highnefs offered to take him into his fervice, and fend him to Italy, for the completion of his Mufical ftudies; but his father declining this honour, from a fpirit of independence, it was determined that he fhould return to Halle, where he muft have continued a confiderable

(a) The earl of Marchmont, in his travels through Germany, when Lord Polwarth, picked them up as great curiofities, and gave them to Mr. Weideman, of whom he took leffons on the German flute. A friend, who favoured me with this anecdote, procured a copy of thefe juvenile productions, which are now in his Majefty's collection, and which Weideman fhewed to HANDEL; who feemed to look at them with much plea-fure, and laughing, faid, " I ufed to write like the D——l in thofe days, but chiefly for the hautbois, which was my favourite inftrument." This, and the having fuch an exquifite performer to write for, as San Martini, accounts for the frequent opportunities which HANDEL took of compofing for that inftrument, in the early part of his life.

B 2

time;

time; though we are told that his father's death happening soon after his return from Berlin, HANDEL, not being able to support the expence of a journey to Italy, whither he was ambitious of going, removed to Hamburgh, in order, by his musical talents, to procure a subsistence: this city, next to Berlin, being then the most renowned for its operas. We lose sight, however, in all the accounts of his life hitherto published, both of our young Musician and his improvements from the time of his quitting Berlin, till his arrival at Hamburgh, a period of five years; for, according to his rival Matthefon, he did not visit that city till the year 1703, at the age of nineteen.

Yet the celebrated *Telemann*, one of the greatest German Musicians of his time, in a well-written account of his own life and works, drawn up by himself at the request of Matthefon, in the year 1740, furnishes two or three incidents concerning HANDEL, which intervened between the time of his quitting Berlin and arrival at Hamburgh, that will help to throw a little light on this dark period of his history.

Telemann, born at Magdeburgh 1681 *(a)*, like HANDEL, discovered an early passion for Music, and, while he was at school, had, like him, made a great progress in the art, contrary to the inclination of his friends; but though he played on almost every kind of instrument, and had attempted to compose an opera at twelve years old, yet, in obedience to his mother's positive commands, on whom, as his father was dead, he was solely dependent, at about the age of twenty he solemnly renounced his musical pursuits, though with the greatest reluctance, and set out for Leipsic, in order to study the law in that university. In the way thither,

_____

(a) See *Germ. Tour*, vol. ii. p. 242.

how-

however, he ftopt at *Halle*, where, fays Telemann, " from my
" acquaintance with HANDEL, who was *already famous*, I again
" fucked in fo much of the poifon of mufic as nearly overfet all
" my refolutions."

HANDEL was now but fixteen years of age ; and as Telemann,
in his account of himfelf and his ftudies, foon mentions our juvenile Mufician again, I fhall proceed a little further in his narrative.

" However," continues Telemann, " after quitting HANDEL,
" I perfevered in the plan prefcribed by my mother, and went to
" Leipfic to purfue my ftudies ; but, unfortunately, was lodged
" in a houfe where I perpetually heard Mufic of all kinds, which,
" though much worfe than my own, again led me into tempta-
" tion. And a fellow-ftudent finding among my papers a pfalm
" which I had fet to mufic, and which, in facrificing all my other
" illicit attempts at compofition, had chanced to efcape oblivion,
" he begged it of me, and had it performed at St. Thomas's
" church, where it was fo much approved, that the burgomafter
" defired I would compofe fomething of this kind every fort-
" night ; for this I was amply rewarded, and had hopes, like-
" wife, given me, of future advantages of much greater import-
" tance. At this time I happened to be reminded of the folemn
" promife I had made my mother, for whom I had a great reve-
" rence, of utterly abandoning all thoughts of Mufic, by receiv-
" ing from her a draught for my fubfiftence : which, however,
" I returned ; and, after mentioning the profitable and promifing
" ftate of my affairs, earneftly intreated her to relax a little in the
" rigour of her injunctions, concerning the ftudy of Mufic. Her
" bleffings on my new labours, followed ; and now I was half a
" mufician again.

" Soon

" Soon after I was appointed director of the opera, for which
" I compoſed many dramas, not only for Leipſic, where I eſta-
" bliſhed the College of Muſic which ſtill ſubſiſts, but for So-
" rau, Frankfort, and the court of Weiſſenfels. The organ of the
" new church was then juſt built, of which I was appointed or-
" ganiſt and director of the Muſic.   This organ, however, I only
" played at the conſecration, or opening, and afterwards reſigned
" it, as a bone of contention for young muſical ſtudents to quarrel
" and ſcramble for.   At this time the pen of the excellent Kuh-
" nau ſerved me for a model in fugue and counterpoint ; but in
" faſhioning ſubjects of melody, HANDEL *and I were continually*
" *exerciſing our fancy, and reciprocally communicating our thoughts,*
" *both by letter and converſation, in the frequent viſits we made to*
" *each other (a)*".

According to Telemann's dates, all this muſt have happened
between the year 1701 and 1703, when HANDEL, quitting Halle,
arrived at Hamburgh, a place too diſtant from Leipſic for frequent
viſits between theſe young Muſicians to have been practicable *(b)*.

It is ſo difficult to obtain authentic intelligence concerning the
tranſactions of individuals, in remote parts of the world ; that,
finding how ſeldom foreigners ſpeak accurately of what happens in
our own country, when we ſpeak of theirs, I cannot help ſuſpect-
ing myſelf, as well as others, of ſimilar ignorance and inaccuracy.

In the accounts of our Theatres, by Riccoboni ; of our Poets
by Quadrio ; and of our Muſic by Mattheſon, and others, the
information is ſo ſcanty and erroneous, that nothing can be more
contemptible than the ſituation into which we are placed in the
eyes of our neighbours by theſe accounts, unleſs it be the authors

(*a*) Mattheſon's 𝕰𝔥𝔯𝔢𝔫 𝔓𝔣𝔬𝔯𝔱𝔢, p. 354.   (*b*) Leipſic, which is only 24 Engliſh
1740.   miles from Halle, is 200 from Hamburgh.

them-

themfelves, in the opinion of thofe who are able to detect their miftakes.

The difficulty of eradicating error when it has once gained admiffion into books, has been long obferved ; as it is much more eafy to take facts for granted and implicitly tranfcribe, than to examine and confute them.

HANDEL having paffed his youth on the continent, and chiefly in Germany, the incidents of that part of his life muft have been better known by his cotemporary countrymen than by an inhabitant of England, who, at the diftance of fifty years from the arrival of this great Mufician among us, depended on tradition for facts.

John Matthefon, an able Mufician and voluminous writer on the fubject of Mufic, who refided at Hamburgh during the whole time that HANDEL remained in that city, has many particulars difperfed through his writings, which merit attention. For though he fometimes appears as a friend, companion, and admirer of HANDEL's genius and abilities, and at others affumes the critic, difcovering manifeft figns of rivalry, envy, and difcontent, at his fuperior fuccefs ; yet, Matthefon was never fo abandoned a writer as to invent or difguife facts, which he knew the whole city of Hamburgh, and even HANDEL himfelf, who was living till within five years of this author's death, could confute *(a)*.

(a) When I firft began this *Sketch*, feveral of Matthefon's Mufical Tracts in my poffeffion having been miflaid, I was unable to confult them ; but being fince found, refpect for my readers, and for truth, have induced me to cancel feveral leaves that were already printed, and to new write this part of HANDEL's Life, in order not only to correct the miftakes into which I had been led by trufting to his former Englifh Biographer, but to infert from German writers fuch other incidents as concern HANDEL's younger years, of which, as we know but little in England, the admirers of this venerable mafter will be more particularly curious.

MAT-

MATTHESON, born at Hamburgh 1681, had a liberal educa-
tion, and became a confiderable perfonage in that city; where, in
the younger part of his life, he figured in the triple capacity of compofer, opera-finger, and harpfichord-player: and afterwards, though
he quitted the ftage upon being appointed fecretary to Sir Cyril
Wych, the Englifh refident, yet he continued to ftudy, practife,
and write on Mufical fubjects, till the time of his death.

He difcovered as early a propenfity to Mufic as Telemann or
HANDEL: having been able at nine years old to fing his own
compofitions to the organ, in one of the Hamburgh churches;
and, at eighteen, he fet an opera called the *Pleiades*, for the theatre
in that city, in which he fung the principal part himfelf.

Indeed, Matthefon's early connexion and intercourfe there with
HANDEL, before his name as a great Mufician had penetrated
into other parts of Europe, were fuch, that it is hopelefs now to
feek for better information than his writings furnifh, concerning
fo interefting a period.

Matthefon was a vain and pompous man, whofe firft wifh in
all his writings was to imprefs the reader with due reverence for
his own abilities and importance *(a)*. It was his boaft before his
death, in 1764, at the age of eighty-three, ' that he had printed
' as many books, on the fubject of Mufic, as he had lived years;
' and that he fhould leave to his executors an equal number, in
' manufcript for the ufe of pofterity.

' In 1761, he publifhed a Tranflation of the Life of HANDEL,
' from the Englifh; with additions and remarks, which are nei-
' ther very candid nor liberal. But how fhould the author of that

---

(a) In this he feems to have fucceeded
with his countrymen, as feveral theoretical
books are dedicated to him: and Mr. Marpurg's *Treatife on Thorough-Bafe*, among
the reft. Handuch bey dem General-
baffe und der Compofition. Berlin, 1762.

' book

' book expect quarter from him, in which it is afferted, that " Mat-
" thefon was no great finger, and only employed occafionally." In
' refutation of which he affures us, " that he conftantly fung the
" principal parts in the Hamburgh operas, during fifteen years,
" and with fuch fuccefs, that he could command the paffions of
" his audience, by exciting in them, at his pleafure, joy, grief,
" hope, and fear." And who fhall venture to doubt of his
' having poffeffed thefe powers, when their effects are thus at-
' tefted *by himfelf (a) ?*'

In a work of Mufical biography and criticifm, by Matthefon,
called 𝕲𝖗𝖚𝖓𝖉𝖑𝖆𝖌𝖊 𝖊𝖎𝖓𝖊𝖗 𝕰𝖍𝖗𝖊𝖓=𝕻𝖋𝖔𝖗𝖙𝖊, *Foundation of a triumphal
Arch*, in honour of Mufic and Muficians, publifhed at Hamburgh, 1740, in which there is a long and inflated account of
himfelf and his works, which occupies thirty pages, we have, as
well as in his annotations on the Englifh Life, a more ample and
fatisfactory account of HANDEL's juvenile compofitions and ad-
ventures, than I have been able to find elfewhere.

After telling us that he arrived at Hamburgh in the fummer of
1703, rich in genius and good difpofition : " Here," fays Matthefon, " almoft his firft acquaintance was myfelf; as I met with
" him at the organ of St. Mary Magdalen's church, July the
" 30th, whence I conducted him to my father's houfe, where he
" was treated with all poffible kindnefs as well as hofpitality; and
" I afterwards not only attended him to organs, choirs, operas,
" and concerts, but recommended him to feveral fcholars, par-
" ticularly to one in a certain houfe, where every body was
" much devoted to Mufic *(b)*.

(*a*) *Journal of a Mufical Tour through Germany,* &c. vol ii.

(*b*) This appears, in another of Mat-thefon's works, to have been the houfe of the Englifh refident, where it feems as if he had fupplanted HANDEL before his depar-ture from Hamburgh, by being appointed, not only *Secretaire de Legation*, and Gover-nor to the Refident's fon, but his Mufic-mafter.

* B   " At

" At firſt he only played a *ripieno* violin in the opera orcheſtra,
" and behaved as if he could not count five; being naturally in-
" clined to dry humour *(a)*.

" At this time he compoſed extreme long Airs and Cantatas
" without end; of which, though the harmony was excellent,
" yet true taſte was wanting; which, however, he very ſoon
" acquired by his attendance at the opera."

As theſe young Muſicians lived much together in great intimacy, they had frequent amicable conteſts and trials of ſkill with
each other; in which it appearing that they excelled on different
inſtruments, HANDEL on the organ, and Mattheſon on the harp-
ſichord, they mutually agreed not to invade each other's province,
and faithfully obſerved this compact for five or ſix years.

Mattheſon tells us, that in the year 1704, the opera-houſe at
Hamburgh happening to be ſhut, leaving HANDEL behind him,
he travelled to Holland, played on the famous organs, and heard the
great performers in that country; made concerts at Amſterdam,
and might have been elected organiſt of Haerlem: having had an
offer of that place, with a ſalary of fifteen hundred Dutch goldens,
equal to near a hundred and fifty pounds ſterling a year. He had then
thoughts of going to England, but was prevented from executing
that deſign, or of accepting the place of organiſt at Haerlem, by
the preſſing intreaties he received from the managers of the opera,
his family, friends, and confeſſor; but chiefly by a moſt kind and
obliging letter which was written to him by HANDEL, from
Hamburgh. This letter in order to ſhew the kind of intimacy

(a) " I know," ſays Mattheſon, " if " cook's ſon who blew the bellows for us at
" he happens to read this, he will laugh in " St. Mary's; our parties on the water to-
" his heart, for he never laughed outward- " gether; and a hundred other circum-
" ly; particularly if he remembers the poul- " ſtances, ſtill freſh in my mind."
" terer who travelled with us; the paſtry-

which

which then fubfifted between them, Mattheson has inferted in his *Triumphal Arch*.   It is dated March 18, and was written before clafhing interefts and rival claims had occafioned any interruption to their friendfhip; among other expreffions of civility from HANDEL, he gives the following.

" I often wifh to enjoy your very agreeable converfation, which " I hope will foon happen, as the time approaches, when, without " your prefence, nothing can be done at the opera.   I moft hum-" bly intreat you to inform me of your departure from Amfter-" dam, that I may have an opportunity of fhewing my regard, by " giving you the meeting."

HANDEL, at this time, muft have been compofing his firft Opera, in which, depending upon Mattheson to perform the principal man's part, he had, probably, fet the fongs to his ftyle of finging and compafs of voice; but vanity never fuffered Mat-thefon to afcribe HANDEL's attentions to any thing but pure love and kindnefs.

In his remarks on the Englifh Life of HANDEL, he is parti-cularly fevere on that part of it which contains an account of the quarrel which happened between him and that compofer, foon after the letter was written: accufing the Biographer not only of violating geography, chronology, and hiftory, but of a wilful mifreprefentation of facts, in relating the circumftances of this breach between them.

Mattheson, who, with all his felf-complaifance and pedantry, is generally allowed to have been diligent in finding, and exact in ftating facts, after telling us that HANDEL, when he firft came to Hamburgh, notwithftanding the exalted ftation at which he foon arrived, had no better part affigned him in the opera, than the

Second ripieno Violin (a); informs us, that " though he then pre-
" tended to know nothing, yet he ufed to be very arch, for he
" had always a dry way of making the gravest people laugh, with-
" out laughing himfelf.   But his fuperior abilities were foon dif-
" covered, when, upon occafion of the harpfichord-player at
" the opera being abfent, he was firft perfuaded to take his
" place; for he then fhewed himfelf to be a great mafter, to the
" aftonifhment of every one, except myfelf, who had frequently
" heard him before, upon keyed-inftruments."

According to Matthefon's own confeffion, he acquired from
HANDEL, by frequently meeting him at his father's houfe, and
practifing with him, a knowledge of modulation, and method of
combining founds, which he could have learned of no one elfe.

Upon a vacancy in an organift's place at Lubec, they travelled
thither together, and in the *wagen* compofed feveral double
fugues, *da mente*, fays Matthefon, not *da penna*. Buxtehude
was then at Lubec, and an admirable organ-player; however,
HANDEL's powers on that inftrument aftonifhed even thofe who
were accuftomed to hear that great performer. HANDEL and
Matthefon were prevented from becoming candidates for the place
of organift at Lubec, by a condition that was annexed to the
obtaining that office; which was no other than to take with it,
a wife, whom their conftituents were to nominate; but thinking
this too great an honour, they precipitately retreated to Hamburgh.

About this time an opera, called *Cleopatra*, compofed by Matthefon, was performed on that ftage, in which he acted the part of
Anthony himfelf, and HANDEL played the harpfichord; but Mat-

(a) " To how minute an origin we owe
" Young Ammon, Cæfar, and the great Naffau !"

thefon

thefon being accuftomed, upon the death of Anthony, which happens early in the piece, to take the harpfichord, in the character of compofer, HANDEL refufed to indulge his vanity, by relinquifhing to him this poft; which occafioned fo violent a quarrel between them, that at going out of the houfe, Matthefon gave him a flap on the face; upon which, both immediately drew their fwords, and a duel enfued in the Market-place, before the door of the Opera-houfe: luckily, the fword of Matthefon was broke againft a metal button upon HANDEL's coat, which put an end to the combat, and they were foon after reconciled.

Such is the account, which, long before the death of HANDEL, Matthefon himfelf publifhed, concerning the difference that happened between them, during his refidence at Hamburgh.

The Englifh biographer is very roughly handled by Matthefon for faying, that this duel had " more the appearance of *affaffina-* " *tion* than of a *rencounter*," and accufes him of conftantly and wilfully diminifhing the age of HANDEL, in order to reprefent him not only as a prodigy in Mufic, but a youth of too tender years to be poffeffed of courage, reafon, or fkill, fufficient to defend himfelf; but if he had been capable of making a defence, fays the author of his Life, " he could not be prepared for it." In anfwer to all this, Matthefon obferves, that " HANDEL, at the " time of the quarrel, was twenty years of age; tall, ftrong, " broad-fhouldered, and mufcular; confequently, well able to de- " fend himfelf:" and adds, that " *a dry flap on the face was no* " *affaffination, but rather a friendly hint, to put him on his guard.*"

This rencounter happened the 5th of December, 1704; and, as a proof of a fpeedy reconciliation, Matthefon tells us, that on the 30th of the fame month, he accompanied the young compofer to the rehearfal of his firft opera of *Almira*, at the theatre, and

per-

performed in it the principal part; and that, afterwards, they became greater friends than ever. This opera, though rehearſed at the end of 1704, was not publicly performed till the beginning of 1705, when it was greatly approved *(a)*.

On the 25th of February of the ſame year, he produced his ſecond opera, called *Nero*, which had likewiſe a very favourable reception *(b)*. It was at the end of the run of theſe two dramas that Mattheſon, who performed the principal man's part in both, quitted the ſtage, on his being appointed ſecretary to the Britiſh reſident at Hamburgh; an office in which he continued to the time of his death, at the diſtance of near ſixty years from his firſt appointment *(c)*.

That Mattheſon had more knowledge than taſte, no other proof need be given than the following conceit, which was related to me at Hamburgh. Late in life, in ſetting, as part of his own funeral anthem, the third verſe of the fourth chapter of Revelations: " And there was a *rain-bow* round about the throne," he contrived in a very full ſcore, to make every part form an *arch*, by a gradual aſcent and deſcent of the notes on paper, in plain counter-point; which appearance to the *eyes* of the performers, he probably thought would convey the idea of a *rain-bow* to the *ears* of the congregation !

(*a*) The German title of this opera is: Der in Kronen erlangte Glückſwechſel, oder Almira, Koeniginn von Caſtilien; that is, *The Viciſſitudes of Royalty*, or ALMIRA *Queen of Caſtile*. There was an Epilogue to this drama, called *The Genius of Europe*, ſet by Keyſer.

(*b*) This opera was ſtyled in German: Nero, oder die durch Blut und Mord erlangte liebe ; NERO, or, *Love obtained by Blood and Murder*.

(*c*) Mattheſon's firſt opera, called the *Pleiades*, was performed at Hamburgh, 1699. *Porſenna*, the ſecond, 1702. *Victor, Duke of Normandy*, the third, of which Schieferdecker compoſed the firſt act, Mattheſon the ſecond, and Bronner the third, was performed the ſame year. *Cleopatra*, the fourth, which occaſioned the quarrel between Mattheſon and HANDEL, 1704.

All

All the Mufic that I have ever feen by Matthefon is fteril of ideas and uninterefting. It has been faid, that he was a great, performer on the harpfichord, and that HANDEL frequently amufed himfelf with playing his pieces; in doing which, if ever he regarded Matthefon as a formidable rival, his triumph muft have been very complete in comparing them with his own, or with the inherent powers which he muft have felt of producing better whenever he pleafed. I am in poffeffion of a fet of Twelve Leffons by Matthefon, engraved on copper, by Fletcher, in tall folio of eighteen ftaved paper, London 1714; who, in a Preface fpeaks of them as " Pieces which claim precedence to all others " of this nature; as being compofed by one of the greateft maf- " ters of the age, in a tafte altogether pleafing and fublime." They confift of *Overtures*, *Preludes*, *Fugues*, *Allemandes*, *Cou-rantes*, *Gigues* and *Aires*; but, notwithftanding the Editor's Eloge, like all the harpfichord mufic I ever faw, anterior to HANDEL's admirable *Suites de Pieces*, firft Set, 1720; though in good harmony, it impreffes the mind with no better idea of accent, grace, or paffion, than the gingling of triangles, or bells of a pack-horfe; and is truly fuch as degrades the inftrument to the level of *founding brafs and a tinkling cymbal*.

From 1705 to 1708, when HANDEL fet two other operas, *Florindo* and *Dafne*, he furnifhed nothing for the ftage; though he had many fcholars, compofed harpfichord-pieces, fingle fongs, and cantatas, innumerable *(a)*.

During

(a) I procured at Hamburgh, in 1773, a manufcript collection of cantatas, by the principal compofers of the early part of the prefent century; among which are two by HANDEL, which I never faw elfewhere; and thefe, it is moft probable, were pro-duced in that city, during his refidence there, previous to his arrival in England, or journey into Italy. One of thefe can-tatas has a fpirited accompaniment for a harpfichord, *obligato*. At the end is a fhort air, which feems to contain the germ, or fubject, of a favourite harpfichord leffon, printed in the fecond volume of his *Pieces de*

Cla-

During his refidence at Hamburgh, Matthefon allows, that HANDEL improved his own ftyle greatly, by his conftant attendance at the opera; and fays, that he was even more powerful upon the organ, in extempore fugues and counterpoint, than the famous Kuhnau of Leipfic, who was at this time regarded as a prodigy.

HANDEL having acquired by his operas at Hamburgh a fum fufficient to enable him to vifit Italy, fet out for that feat of the Mufes, a journey after which every man of genius fo ardently pants. He ftaid fome time at Florence, where he compofed the opera of *Rodrigo*. From this city he went to Venice, where, in 1709, he produced his *Agrippina*, which is faid by his biographer to have been received with acclamation, and to have run thirty nights. Here he met with Domenico Scarlatti, Gafparini, and Lotti.

The next place he vifited, was Rome, where he had an opportunity of hearing compofitions and performers of the firft clafs. Here the elder Scarlatti and Gafparini had brought vocal mufic to great perfection, and Corelli, inftrumental. At cardinal Ottoboni's, by whom HANDEL was greatly careffed and patronized, he had frequently the advantage of hearing the natural and elegant Corelli perform his own works. Here our young compofer produced a ferenata: *Il Trionfo del Tempo (a)* ; after which he proceeded to Naples, where he fet *Acis and Galatea*, in Italian, to mufic totally different from the little Englifh drama, written by Gay, which he fet in 1721, for the duke of Chandos.

Clavecin, p. 5, the identical movement with which he ended the laft concerto which he ever played in public. This cantata is the more likely to have been compofed early in his youth, as there are fome little liberties, and negligences in the compofition, which have never appeared in his later productions.

(a) The original fcore of this work is in his Majefty's collection. In 1770, I pur-chafed at Rome, among other manufcript compofitions by old mafters, fix cantatas, *a voce Sola*, del Georgio Federigo HENDEL, *detto il Saffone*, which were, probably, produced in this city during his refidence there, about the year 1709: by the yellow colour of the ink, they feem to have been long tranfcribed. Some of them I have never feen in any other collection.

When he returned to Germany, on quitting Italy, at the latter end of 1709, or the beginning of 1710, the firſt place at which he ſtopt was Hanover; where he found a munificent patron in the Elector, who afterwards, on the death of queen Anne, aſcended the Engliſh throne, by the name of George the Firſt. This prince had in his ſervice, as maeſtro di capella, the elegant and learned compoſer Steffani, whom HANDEL had met before at Venice, and who now reſigned his office of maeſtro di capella to the Elector, in his favour. This venerable compoſer ſerved him as a model for the ſtyle of chamber duets, as well as facilitated his introduction to the ſmiles of his patron, the Elector, who ſet-tled on him a penſion of 1500 crowns, upon condition that he would return to his court, when he had completed his travels. HANDEL, acceding to this propoſition, went to Duſſeldorp, where he had a flattering reception from the Elector Palatine, who, likewiſe, wiſhed to retain him in his ſervice. But beſides the en-gagement into which he had entered with the Elector of Hanover, he was impatient to viſit England, where a paſſion for dramatic Muſic had already manifeſted itſelf in ſeveral aukward at-tempts at operas, and to which place he had received invitations from ſeveral of the nobility, whom he had ſeen in Italy and Ha-nover.

It was at the latter end of the year 1710, that he arrived in England; his reception was as flattering to himſelf as honourable to the nation, at this time no leſs ſuccefsful in war, than in the cultivation of the arts of peace. To the wit, poetry, literature, and ſcience, which marked this period of our hiſtory, HANDEL added all the blandiſhments of a nervous and learned Muſic, which he firſt brought hither, planted, and lived to ſee grow to a very flouriſhing ſtate.

C   Of

Of the fuperior talents and abilities, which HANDEL now poffeffed, and of the fuccefs with which he had exercifed both on the Continent, Fame, who in the character of *avant-coureur*, had wafted intelligence to this country, procured him an eafy and favourable reception at court, and in many of the principal families of the kingdom. Aaron Hill, at this time manager of the opera, availing himfelf of his arrival, haftily fketched out the plan of a Mufical Drama, from Taffo's Jerufalem, and gave it to the Italian poet, Roffi, to work into an opera, by the name of RINALDO. This Drama was firft performed in March 1711, and HANDEL is faid, in the Preface, to have fet it to Mufic *in a fortnight*.

Mr. Addifon, in the Spectator, N° 5, with his ufual pleafantry, but total infenfibility to fuperior mufical excellence, mentions this circumftance among other frivolous incidents, which he means to ridicule. Had this writer and critic, fo admirable in other refpects, been poffeffed of judgment and feeling in Mufic equal to his learning and tafte in literature, he would have difcovered that to compofe an entire opera in lefs time than a copyift could tranfcribe it, and in a more mafterly and original ftyle than had ever before been heard in this, or perhaps, any country, was not a fair fubject for farcafm. All Mufic feems alike to Addifon, except French Recitative, for which he feems to have a particular predilection *(a)*.

The opera of *Rinaldo*, in which the celebrated Nicolini and Valentini, the firft Italian fingers that appeared on our ftage, performed; was the delight of the nation during many years : as it was revived 1712, 1717, and 1731.

After remaining about a year in this country, and eftablifhing a great reputation on the folid bafis of the moft exalted and indif-

(a) *Spectator*, N° 29.

putable

putable merit, both as a compofer and performer, he returned to Hanover, on a promife made to his moft powerful Englifh friends to revifit this kingdom again, as foon as he could obtain per- miffion of his Electoral Highnefs and patron. About the end of the year 1712, this permiffion was granted for a limited time. And we find his *Paftor Fido*, and *Thefeus*, in the lift of Italian operas, brought on the Englifh ftage, this and the following year. And in 1715, *Amadige*, or *Amadis of Gaul*. In all thefe operas Nicolini, Valentini, Margarita, and Mrs. Anaftafia Robinfon, were the principal fingers.

Not long after his fecond arrival in London, the peace of Utrecht having been brought to a conclufion, HANDEL was pre- ferred to all others, feemingly without a murmur from native Muficians, to compofe the Hymn of Gratitude and Triumph on the occafion. Envy, though outrageous and noify at the fuccefs of comparative abilities, is ftruck dumb and blind by excefs of fuperiority. The grand *Te Deum* and *Jubilate*, which he fet on this occafion, were compofed with fuch force, regularity, and in- ftrumental effects, as the Englifh had never heard before. Purcell's *Te Deum*, in defign, and expreffion of the words, is, perhaps, fuperior to all others ; but in grandeur and richnefs of accompa- niment, nothing but national partiality can deny HANDEL the preference. The queen fettled on him for life a penfion of Two Hundred pounds per annum. And all who had heard Rinaldo, wifhed him again employed for the opera ; fo that the multiplicity of bufinefs, and the many protectors and friends he met with in England, a little impaired the memory of our great compofer with refpect to continental connections ; and he feemed to think of nothing lefs than returning to Hanover till after the death of queen Anne, in 1714, when his majefty, George the Firft,

arriving

arriving in England, faved him the trouble of a German tour.

HANDEL, confcious of his deficiency in refpect and gratitude, to a prince who honoured him with fuch flattering marks of approbation and bounty, durft not approach the court, till by the ingenuity and friendly interpofition of baron Kilmanfegge, he was reftored to favour in the following manner. The king, foon after his arrival in thefe kingdoms, having been prevailed on to form a party on the water, the defign was communicated to HANDEL, who was advifed to compofe fome pieces exprefsly for the occafion; the performance of which he fecretly conducted in a boat, that accompanied the royal barge. Upon hearing thefe compofitions, which have been fince fo well known, and fo juftly celebrated under the title of the *Water-Mufic*, his majefty, equally furprifed and pleafed by their excellence, eagerly enquired who was the author of them; when the baron acquainted the king that they were the productions of a faithful fervant of his majefty, who, confcious of the caufe of difpleafure which he had given to fo gracious a protector, durft not prefume to approach his royal prefence, till he had affurances that by every poffible demonftration of duty and gratitude in future, he might hope to obtain a pardon. This interceffion having been gracioufly accepted, HANDEL was reftored to favour, and his compofitions honoured with the moft flattering marks of royal approbation. And as a ratification of the delinquent's peace, thus eafily obtained, his majefty was pleafed to add a penfion of Two Hundred pounds a-year to that which had been previoufly conferred on him by queen Anne; and not many years after, when he was employed to teach the young princeffes, another penfion of the fame value was added to the former grants, by her majefty queen Caroline.

From

From the year 1715 to 1720, I find, in the records of the Mufical Drama, no new opera that was fet by HANDEL. The firſt three years of this period were chiefly ſpent at the earl of Burlington's, a nobleman, whoſe taſte and judgment in the fine arts were as exquiſite as his patronage to their votaries was liberal. And during the other two years, HANDEL ſeems to have been employed at Cannons, as maeſtro di capella to the duke of Chandos; who, among other ſplendid and princely kinds of magnificence, eſtabliſhed a chapel, in which the cathedral ſervice was daily performed by a choir of voices and inſtruments, ſuperior, at that time, perhaps, in number and excellence, to that of any ſovereign prince in Europe. Here HANDEL produced, beſides his anthems, the chief part of his hautbois concertos, ſonatas, leſſons, and organ fugues; which are all ſo maſterly, ſpirited, and exquiſite in their ſeveral kinds, that if he had never compoſed an opera, oratorio, Te Deum, duet, cantata, or any other ſpecies of vocal muſic, his name would have been had in reverence by true Muſicians, as long as the characters in which they are written, ſhould continue to be legible.

We come now to the buſieſt and moſt glorious period of HANDEL's life; who, arrived at that ſtage of exiſtence which Dante calls

Il mezzo del cammin di noſtra vita:

when the human frame and faculties have acquired their utmoſt ſtrength and vigour; was endowed with great natural powers, highly improved by cultivation; with a hand which no difficulties could embarraſs; a genius for compoſition unbounded; at the head of a profeſſion which facilitates acceſs to the great, and, with extraordinary abilities, enſures their patronage; high in the favour of

the

the fovereign, nobles, and public, of a great and powerful nation, at a period of its greateft happinefs and tranquillity ; when it was not only bleft with leifure and zeal to cultivate the arts of peace, but with power, liberally to reward thofe whofe fuccefsful efforts had carried them beyond the bounds of mediocrity.

Such were HANDEL's circumftances and fituation, when a plan was formed, by the Englifh nobility and gentry, for eftablifh- ing a fund for the fupport of Italian operas, of which he was to be the compofer and director ; and, as his Majefty king George the Firft was pleafed to fubfcribe one thoufand pounds towards the execution of this defign, and to let his name appear at the head of the fubfcription, amounting to fifty thoufand pounds, this fo- ciety was called the *Royal Academy.*

When HANDEL quitted his employment at Cannons, he was commiffioned by this academy to go to Drefden, in order to en- gage fingers. Here he found Senefino, Duraftanti, Berenftadt, and Bofchi, whom he brought over to England.

Though the principal intention, in forming the academy, was to appoint HANDEL the compofer and director of the band ; the public was not, as yet, unanimous in fupporting this meafure. Bononcini and Attilio had been invited over by the former mana- gers of the opera ; and as they were compofers of acknowledged merit, there was an unwillingnefs in their admirers and friends to confent to their difmiffion. And it was now that thofe mufical feuds began, of which Swift has perpetuated the memory, by an epigram, which throws contempt upon an art, and upon artifts, whofe merit he never felt or underftood, though he could fee the ridicule of their fituation. But the fatirift who difcovers no dif- ference between a Dryden and a Bell-man, or a Raphael and a Houfe-painter, is full as well qualified to talk about poetry and

painting,

painting, as he about mufic, who neither fees nor hears the difference between the productions of a HANDEL or a Bononcini,
and thofe of the moft defpicable fiddler.

No art, fcience, or even religious or moral truth, can parry the
affaults of ridicule, when wit and humour guide the thruft;
though, luckily, the wounds inflicted are flight, and cure themfelves. For neither lovers of art, nor of religion and virtue, can
be long diverted from their purfuits, by a gibe or *bon mot*. A
great nation, in which there are fo many opulent individuals,
wants innocent amufements for their leifure hours, when quitting
the chace and rural fports they are affembled together in the capital; and in the beft and moft polifhed ages of the world, the cultivation and patronage of Mufic have employed the talents and
munificence of its moft diftinguifhed inhabitants.

Mufical dramas or operas, which during the laft century travelled from Italy to France, and from France to England, were
never attempted in the Italian language till the reign of queen
Anne, when the firft effays were made by performers, partly natives, and partly Italians, who feverally ufed their own dialect;
the abfurdity of which Addifon has ridiculed with great humour
and pleafantry in the Spectator, No. 18 *(a)*. But as the love for
operas was then, and has been ever fince, moft powerfully excited
in fuch of our nobility and gentry as have vifited Italy in their
youth, it is natural that they fhould at all times wifh to have thefe
exhibitions as near the models with which they had been acquainted on the continent, as poffible. And of fuch we may fup-
pofe the Royal Academy was compofed: as the duke of New-

(a) The Germans, according to Riccoboni, at the beginning of this century, had
operas performed in the fame manner; the
Recitative being pronounced in German,
and the Airs in Italian.

caftle,

caſtle, was governor; lord Bingley, deputy-governor; and the dukes of Portland and Queenſbury, earls of Burlington, Stair, and Waldegrave, lords Chetwynd and Stanhope, James Bruce, eſq. colonel Blathwait, Thomas Coke, of Norfolk, eſq. Conyers D'Arcy, eſq. brigadier-general Dormer, Bryan Fairfax, eſq. co-lonel O'Hara, George Harriſon, eſq. brigadier-general Hunter, William Pulteney, eſq. ſir John Vanbrugh, major-general Wade, and Francis Whitworth, eſq. directors.

Theſe great and eminent perſonages could not, however, get the whole management of the operas into their own hands, all at once: oppoſitions are no leſs frequent, than furious, in popular governments; and, on this occaſion, political animoſities were blended with Muſical faction. All the friends of Bononcini and Attilio were not, perhaps, entirely guided by the love of Muſic, and ſenſe of their ſuperiority; the love of power, and hatred of the abettors of HANDEL, for party conſiderations, furniſhed fuel to their zeal; and HANDEL, ere they gave way, was forced to mount the ſtage, and fight his own battle. For all that his friends could obtain of thoſe that were in poſſeſſion of the Theatre in the Haymarket, at his return from Dreſden, with auxiliaries, was permiſſion to have his opera of *Radamiſtus* performed there in 1720 *(a)*. On this occaſion, the expectations which the public had formed of the abilities of HANDEL, from his great reputation, and the ſpecimens he had already given, may be eſtimated by the crouds which aſſembled at the Opera-Houſe doors, when there was no longer any room for their admiſſion. And the applauſe of thoſe who were ſo fortunate as to obtain places, evinced the full gratification of the delight they expected to receive. This

(a) This opera, under the title of *Ze-nobia*, was tranſlated into German, by Mattheſon, and performed to HANDEL's Muſic, in Hamburgh. 1721.

opera,

opera, however, with all its merit and fuccefs, did not obtain for HANDEL a victory fufficiently decifive, to oblige the enemy to quit the field.

After this, as the laft experiment, it was agreed by the friends of the three feveral rivals, that each of them fhould compofe an act of the fame opera, with an overture to each act. The drama fixed upon was *Mutius Scævola*, of which Bononcini fet the firft act, Attilio the fecond, and HANDEL the third ; and this fiery trial determined the point of precedence between him and his competitors : the act in *Mutius Scævola*, which HANDEL compofed, being pronounced fuperior to both the others, and Bononcini's the next in merit.

It was the more honourable to our great Mufician to have vanquifhed fuch a champion as Bononcini, as he was a man of great abilities, and very high in reputation all over Europe. Few, indeed, are able, when the difference is doubtful, to difcriminate and fet a juft value on the nicer fhades of excellence : a grain of partiality or prejudice can then turn the fcale of either fide, when in the hands of the beft judges ; but how fhall ignorance dare to determine, what learning and experience can fcarce difcern ?

The truth is, that Bononcini's peculiar merit in fetting Italian words feems to have been out of the reach of an Englifh audience, and that Italians were alone competent to judge of it ; who fay, that his knowledge in finging and in their language was fuch as rendered his *cantilena*, or melody, more natural and elegant to vocal performers, and his *recitatives* more paffionate, and expreffive of nicer fenfations and inflexions, to every hearer accuftomed to the tones of Italian fpeech, than thofe of his rival ; but in majefty, grandeur, force, fire, and invention, which are not local

D beauties,

beauties, but ftriking and intelligible in all countries, HANDEL was infinitely his fuperior.

From this memorable victory, in 1721, the Royal Academy feems to have been firmly eftablifhed during the fpace of eight or nine years, under the management of HANDEL's moft powerful friends and greateft admirers; who, in appointing him the principal compofer, gave him abfolute dominion over the performers *(a)*.

There were, however, from time to time, feveral operas of Bononcini and Attilio exhibited during this period, on the fame ftage, and by the fame performers, as thofe of HANDEL; perhaps to conciliate parties: the lovers of Mufic are fometimes froward, capricious, and unreafonable, as well as the profeffors. This was never more confpicuous to by-ftanders, than in the violence of party for the two fingers, Cuzzoni and Fauftina, in the year 1727; at which time, though both were excellent performers, in different ftyles, yet fo unwilling was the Englifh public to be pleafed with both, that when the admirers of one of thefe firens began to applaud, thofe of the other were fure to hifs. It feems as impoffible for two fingers of equal merit to tread the fame ftage, *a parte eguale*, as for two people to ride on the fame horfe, without one being behind.

" If the frequenters of Mufical Dramas had not then been
" enemies to their own pleafure, the merit of thefe fingers con-
" fifted of excellencies fo different and diftinct, that they might

---

(a) During this profperous period, after *Radamifto*, and *Muzio Scevola*, HANDEL produced his operas of *Ottone*, *Floridante*, *Flavio*, *Giulio Cefare*, *Tamerlano*, *Rode-* *linda*, *Scipione*, *Aleffandro*, *Ricardo primo*, *Ammeto*, *Siroe*, *Tolomeo*, *Lotario*, *Partenope*, and *Poro*.

have

" have applauded each by turns, and, from their feveral perfec-
" tions, by turns, have received equal delight.

" Unluckily for moderate people, who feek pleafure from ta-
" lents wherever they can be found, the violence of thefe feuds
" has cured all fucceeding managers of the extravagance of en-
" gaging two fingers of the fame fex, at a time, of difputable
" abilities *(a).*"

Dr. Arbuthnot, on occafion of the contefted rights of *fupremacy*
between thefe theatrical principals and their adherents, publifhed,
1728, a *Manifefto*, intitled, " The Devil to pay at St. James's :
" or a full and true account of a moft horrid and bloody battle
" between *Madame Fauftina* and *Madame Cuzzoni.* Alfo a hot
" fkirmifh between *Signor Bofchi* and *Signor Palmerini.* More-
" over, how *Senefino* has taken fnuff, is going to leave the opera,
" and fing pfalms at *Henley's* Oratory *(b).*"

A few years after, a quarrel happened between HANDEL and
Senefino, which broke up the Academy, and was not only injurious to the fortune of our great Compofer, but the caufe of infi-
nite trouble and vexation to him, during the reft of his life.

Dr. Arbuthnot, who was always a very zealous and active friend
to HANDEL, entered the lifts, as his champion, whenever an
opportunity offered of defending his caufe. And, as *ridicule* fupplied him with all kinds of ammunition, and the *pen* was his
moft irrefiftible weapon, he had recourfe to thefe in the contention with Senefino, who had almoft all the great barons of the
realm for his allies. And in this fecond *puny* war, after mutual
complaints of treaties violated, rights infringed, and hoftilities
committed, he publifhed another *Manifefto*, which had for title,

(a) *Journal of a Mufical Tour through*   (b) *Arbuthnot's Mifcellanies,* vol. i. from
Germany, &c. vol. ii. p. 189.   p. 213, to 216.

" Har-

" Harmony in an Uproar: a Letter to GEORGE FREDERICK
" HANDEL, efq. mafter of the Opera-houfe in the Hay-
" market, from *Hurlothrumbo Johnfon,* efq. compofer extraor-
" dinary to all the theatres in Great Britain, excepting that at
" the Haymarket. In which the rights and merits of both
" Operas are properly confidered."

A court is inftituted in this pamphlet for the trial of HANDEL,
who is ordered to hold up his hand, and to anfwer to the following feveral high crimes and mifdemeanors committed upon the
wills and underftandings of the people of this country.

Imprimis, he is charged with having bewitched us for the fpace
of twenty years paft.

Secondly, with moft infolently daring to give us good Mufic
and found Harmony, when we wanted bad.

Thirdly, with moft felonioufly and arrogantly affuming to himfelf an uncontrouled power of pleafing us whether we would or
no; and with often being fo bold as to charm us, when we were
pofitively refolved to be out of humour.

Dr. *Pufhpin* and Dr. *Blue* (Pepufch and Green) accufe him of
not being a graduate in either of the univerfities; and the former of not having read Euclid, or ftudied the Greek modes.
Others of having compofed fuch Mufic as not only puzzled our
parifh clerks and threw out every congregation, but fuch as never
man produced before. Then, as an inftance of his having practifed forcery in this kingdom on his majefty's liege fubjects, and
of bewitching every fenfe we have, it is afferted that there was
not a letter in any one of his public bills but had magic in it;
and that if at any time a fqueak of one of his fiddles, or a tooting
of one of his pipes was to be heard, away danced the whole town,
helter fkelter, crouding, preffing, and fhoving; and happy were
they

they who could be fqueezed to death.   At length the court concludes, that " as *one* Opera is fuch an enormous fource of ex-
" pence, luxury, idlenefs, floth and effeminacy, there could be
" no way fo proper to redrefs thefe grievances, as the fetting up
" *another.*"

The only parts of this ironical letter which feem to be ferious
are printed in Italics, and contain HANDEL's own defence : who,
in anfwer to the crimes with which he was charged by his oppo-
nents is made to fay, " that he was no way to blame in the whole
" affair ; but that when *Senefino* had declared he would leave
" England, he thought himfelf obliged in honour to proceed with
" his contract, and provide for himfelf elfewhere ; that as for
" *Cuzzoni,* he had no thought of her, no hopes of her, nor no
" want of her, *Strada* being in all refpects infinitely fuperior,
" in any excellency required for the ftage ; as for fingers in the
" under parts, he had provided the beft fet we ever had yet ;
" though bafely deferted by *Montagnana,* after having figned a
" formal contract to ferve him the whole of this feafon ; which
" he might ftill force him to do were he not more afraid of
" Weftminfter-hall than ten thoufand D—rs, or ten thoufand
" D—ls.   That as he was obliged to carry on operas this win-
" ter, he imagined he might be at liberty to proceed in the bufi-
" nefs in that manner which would prove moft to the fatisfaction
" of the unprejudiced part of the nobility and gentry, and his
" own intereft and honour."—He afterwards adds, " that it was
" impoffible for him to comply with the unreafonable and favage
" propofals made to him ; by which he was to give up all con-
" tracts, promifes, nay rifque his fortune, to gratify fantaftical
" whims and unjuft piques."   And continues to plead his own
caufe, by faying, " that if he was mifled, or had judged wrong

D 3   " at

"at any time in raifing the price of his tickets, he was fuffici-
"ently punifhed, without carrying refentment on that account
"to fuch a length *(a)*. But in whatever light the entertain-
"ment was confidered, it certainly better merited fuch an extra-
"vagant price, than any other ever yet exhibited in this na-
"tion."

In another part of this pamphlet, a partizan for HANDEL, captivated by the vocal powers of *Careftini*, whom he had brought over in order to fuperfede *Senefino*, accofts *Hurlothrumbo* in the following manner : "So, Sir, I hear you are a great ftickler for
"the Opera at Lincoln's-Inn-Fields ; a pretty fet of fingers, truly !
"and for compofers, you out-do the world !—Don't you think,
"fays he, at this time of life, *Senefino* could twang a prayer
"finely through the nofe in petticoats at a conventicle ? Hah !
"*(b)*—Or, what think you, fays he, of *Signora Celefti* fnuffling
"a hymn there in concert ; or, *Madame Bertolli*, with her un-
"meaning voice, with as little force in it as a pair of Smith's
"bellows with twenty holes in the fides : Your bafe, indeed *(c)*,

(a) Befides the offence given to the fub-fcribers of the Royal Academy, by refuf-ing to compofe for, or even employ Sene-fino, the great favourite of the nation, HANDEL difobliged them extremely, not only by raifing the price of admiffion to a Guinea, but by refufing to let them occupy their particular boxes in the Haymarket theatre, when he performed there his ora-torio of *Efther*, in the fummer of 1732.

(b) Quadrio has placed Senefino in the lift of fingers who began to diftinguifh themfelves between the year 1690 and 1700; but in examining a collection of more than fifty volumes of Italian operas, or mufical dramas, his name appears in no *Dramatis Perfonæ*, or even Mufical tract, that I have feen, till the year 1719, when he fung the

firft man's part in an opera compofed by Lotti, for the court of the king of Poland, at Drefden, where he was engaged by HANDEL for the Royal Academy in Eng-land. Strange and fudden viciffitudes in human affairs have often excited furprife and exclamation, but in none, I believe, more frequently than in fuch as concern Mufic. Who could have imagined that it would ever become neceffary for HANDEL himfelf, or his friends, to depreciate the talents and *write down* SENESINO, whofe voice, action, tafte, and abilities, had hitherto been the props of his fame and fortune ! But hif-tory fhews that many a fovereign has been greatly incommoded by the defertion and refentment of a difcarded general.

(c) *Montagnana.*

"makes

" makes a humming noise, and could roar to some purpose, if
" he had songs proper for him : as for your *Signora Fagotto (a)*,
" she, indeed, may, with her master, be sent home to school
" again ; and by the time she is fourscore, she'll prove a vast
" addition to a bonfire ; or make a fine Duenna in a Spanish
" opera.

　" Your composers too have behaved notably truly ; your *Por-*
" *poise (b)*, says he, may roul and rumble about as he pleases,
" and prelude to a storm of his own raising ; but you should let
" him know, that a bad imitation always wants the air and spirit
" of an original, and that there is a wide difference betwixt full
" harmony, and making a noise.—I know your expectations are
" very high from the performance of the king of *Arragon (c)* ;
" but that *Trolly Colly* composer, a stupid *cantata-thrummer*,
" must make a mighty poor figure in an opera ; though he was
" so nice last winter, that he would not allow that HANDEL
" could compose, or *Senesino* sing : what art he has used, to pro-
" duce him now as the first voice in Europe, I cannot imagine ;
" but you must not depend upon his majesty too far ; for to my
" knowledge, he has been engaged by a formal deputation from
" the general assembly of North Britain, to new-set their Scotch
" Psalms, and to be clerk to the high-kirk in Edinburgh, with
" a salary of one hundred pounds Scots, per annum."

　This Letter, dated February 12, 1733, was published in a
Shilling pamphlet, and occupies twenty-four pages in the second
volume of Arbuthnot's Miscellanies.　Some of the irony and hu-

(a) *Segatti*, the first woman in the opera established by the nobility in Lincoln's-Inn-Fields, till the second arrival of *Cuzzoni*.

(b) *Porpora.*
(c) *Arrigoni*, the Lutenist.

mour

mour is well pointed, and much of the mufical politics of the day may be gathered from its perufal. As here, we fee who fided with the nobility, when they fet up an opera againft HANDEL in Lincoln's-Inn-Fields, and engaged Porpora and Arrigoni to com-pofe, and placed Senefino and Segatti, till the arrival of Cuzzoni, at the head of the fingers. It appears here, likewife, that Mon-tagnana, the celebrated bafe-finger, Celefte, and Bertolli, two of HANDEL's female performers, as well as Arrigoni, the lu-tenift, with Rolli (*Rowley Powley*) the Italian opera poet, had deferted from his ftandard; and that Dr. Pepufch, Dr. Green, and Holcombe (Mr. *Honeycomb*), were on the fide of the oppo-nents; while Careftini, Strada, the Negri family, Duraftanti and Scalzi, were at the head of his own troop.

It is now too late to determine who was the aggreffor in this long and ruinous war; perhaps HANDEL exercifed his power too roughly, and Senefino was too impatient of controul *(a)*. Per-haps too, the nobility carried their refentment too far, in fetting up another opera to the ruin of a man of fuch uncommon worth and abilities; and, perhaps, if HANDEL's temper had at all re-fembled his finger, in flexibility, a reconciliation might have been effected on no very mortifying or difhonourable terms. It is painful to dwell on this part of his life, which was one continued tiffue of loffes and misfortunes. He produced thirty operas between the year 1721 and 1740; yet, after the diffolution of the Academy, in 1729, none were attended with the fuccefs that was due to their intrinfic and fuperior merit, though

(a) It is related by Quantz, in the Me-moirs of his own Life, that Senefino had a quarrel with Heinechen, the king of Po-land's maeftro di capella, in 1719, which broke up the troop, and was the occafion of his coming to England. *Germ. Tour,* vol. ii. p. 176.

fome

fome of the beft were pofterior to that period. Neglect and oppofition confpired to rob him at once of health, fame, and fortune !

Indeed the breach with the Academy and enmity to Senefino, may with truth be faid to have had fome effect on his later Dramatic compofitions. Senefino had fo noble a voice and manner of finging, was fo admirable an actor, and in fuch high favour with the public, that befides the real force and energy of his performance, there was an additional weight and importance given to whatever he fung, by the elevated fituation in which he ftood with the audience.   I have been acquainted with feveral mafters, and perfons of judgment and probity, who perfectly remembering his performance and its effects on themfelves and the public, affured me, that none of the great fingers, who have fince vifited this country, ever gave fuch exquifite pleafure and heart-felt fatisfaction as Senefino ; who, without high notes or rapid execution, by the majefty and dignity of his perfon, geftures, voice, and expreffion, captivated more, though he furprifed lefs, than Farinelli, Caffarelli, Conti detto Gizziello, Careftini, or any of their immediate fucceffors.   It is impoffible for a compofer to fet a fong to mufic without thinking of the talents and abilities of the finger who is to perform it, and cafting the air in his particular caliber.

The fingers engaged and employed by HANDEL, after the fchifm of Senefino, brought over a new ftyle of finging, and were poffeffed of vocal feats of activity to which he was never partial; it has, however been, I think, unjuftly faid, that the operas he compofed after the quarrel " have fo little to recommend them, " that few would take them for the work of the fame author." Can that fevere fentence be reconciled to judgment, truth, and

can-

candour, in speaking of *Lotharius*, *Ariadne*, *Alcina*, *Berenice*, *Ariodante*, *Xerxes*, and *Faramond?* The voice part of his songs was generally proportioned to the abilities of his singers, and it must be owned, that, with a few exceptions, those of his late operas, and oratorios, were not possessed of great powers either of voice, taste, expression, or execution *(a)*. Yet so unbounded were his orchestra resources, that he never failed making judges of Music ample amends for deficiencies of voice or talents in a singer, by the richness and ingenuity of his accompaniments. And it may, perhaps, be said, that his best *vocal* thoughts, or melodies, seem to have been inspired by the troop for which he composed, in 1727, at the head of which were Senesino, Boschi, Cuzzoni, and Faustina, all possessed of such different kinds of excellence, as might have supported, and sung into favour, the worst Music that ever was composed. There are airs in *Siroe*, which have much merit of a different kind from that which all candid judges readily allow him: for *Non vi piacque ingiusti Dei*, sung by Faustina, and *Deggio morire o stelle*, by Senesino, in that opera, are songs with quiet accompaniments in the style of the most capital modern Airs, in which the singer and the poet are

---

(a) Carestini, Conti detto Gizziello, and *Cafferello,* were all great singers, in a new style of execution, which HANDEL was unwilling to flatter. *Verdi prati*, which was constantly encored during the whole run of *Alcina*, was, at first, sent back to HANDEL by Carestini, as unfit for him to sing; upon which he went, in a great rage, to his house, and in a way which few composers, except HANDEL, ever ventured to accost a *first-singer*, cries out: " You toc! don't I " know better as your seluf, vaat is pest " for you to sing? If you vill not sing all " de song vaat I give you, I vill not pay " you ein stiver."

His government of singers was certainly somewhat despotic: for, upon Cuzzoni insolently refusing to sing his admirable air, *Falsa Imagine*, in *Otho*, he told her that he always knew she was a *very Devil*; but that he should now let *her* know, in her turn, that he was *Beelzebub*, the *Prince of the Devils*. And then, taking her up by the waist, swore, if she did not immediately obey his orders, he would throw her out of the window.

equally

equally refpected. Thefe were compofed in 1728, about the time that Vinci and Haffe had begun to thin and fimplify accompaniment, as well as to polifh melody. In the firft of thefe Airs the voice-part is beautiful and a *canevas* for a great finger; in the fecond, the effects by modulation and broken fentences of melody are truly pathetic and theatrical: the firft violin admirably filling up the chafms in the principal melody, while the fecond violin, tenor, and bafe, are murmuring in the fubdued accompaniment of iterated notes in modern fongs. By thefe two Airs it appears that HANDEL, who had always more folidity and contrivance than his cotemporaries, penetrated very far into thofe regions of tafte and refinement at which his fucceffors only arrived, by a flow progrefs, half a century after.

We fhall now quit his dramatic tranfactions, and confine this narration to fuch incidents as gave rife to the compofition and public performance of his ORATORIOS, which being in our own language, have chiefly endeared him to the nation.

Sacred Dramas, or ORATORIOS, are of great antiquity in Italy, if that title be allowed to the legendary tales, myfteries, and moralities, in which hymns, pfalms, fongs, and chorufes, were incidentally introduced; but the firft regular facred Drama that was wholly fung, and in which the Dialogue was carried on in *Recitative*, was entitled *Anima e Corpo*; it was fet to mufic by Emilio del Cavalieri, and firft performed at Rome, in February, 1600, the fame year as fecular mufical Dramas, or OPERAS, had their beginning at Florence. The Sacred Dramas, which, during the laft century, were performed in the churches and convents of Italy, and generally in action, are innumerable; but the title of ORATORIO was firft given to this fpecies of *Myftery in Mufic*, by

*D

Fran-

Francefco Balducci, about 1645, after which time it became the general term for fuch productions *(a)*. Indeed it appears from the *Drammaturgia* of Italy, that more *Dramme Sacre*, or *Rapprefentazioni Muficali*, on religious fubjects, were performed at Palermo, and, even Naples, during the latter end of the laft century, and beginning of this, than fecular. At the church of *S. Girolamo della Carità*, and *La Chiefa Nuova*, at Rome, Oratorios are ftill conftantly performed on Sundays, from All-Saints day till Palm-Sunday, and on all feftivals; and the confervatorios at Venice are ftill conftant in the ufe of thefe Dramas.

Efther, compofed for the duke of Chandos, in 1720, was the firft Oratorio which HANDEL fet to mufic. And eleven years after its performance at Cannons, a copy of the fcore having been obtained, it was reprefented, in action, by the Children of his Majefty's Chapel, at the houfe of Mr. Bernard Gates, mafter of the boys, in James-ftreet, Weftminfter, on Wednefday, February 23, 1731 *(b)*. The Chorus, confifting of performers from the Chapel-Royal and Weftminfter-Abbey, was placed after the manner of the ancients, between the ftage and orcheftra; and the inftrumental parts were chiefly performed by Gentlemen who were

---

(a) Quadrio, *Storia d'ogna Poefia*, tom. v. p. 495. The word *Oratorio* had its origin from the early introduction of a more artificial kind of mufic than *canto fermo*, or the mafs in a conftant chorus of four parts, at the ORATORY of San Filippo Neri, at Rome, who died 1595.

(b) Dr. Randal of Cambridge, Mr. Beard, and Mr. Barrow, ftill living, were among the children who performed on this occafion.

This Oratorio, and *Athalia*, feem both to have been taken from Racine's two celebrated tragedies of *Efther* and *Athalie*, written for mufic, and performed at the convent of St. Cyr, founded by madame de Maintenon. Nothing, however, but the Chorufes of thefe facred Dramas was ever fung in France, nor was the mufic of thefe Chorufes fet by Lulli, as inadvertently afferted in the former Life of HANDEL. Indeed, Lulli, unluckily, died two years before the firft of thefe tragedies was reprefented; that is, in 1687, and *Efther* was not performed at St. Cyr, till 1689.

mem-

members of the Philarmonic Society. After this, it was performed by the fame fingers at the Crown and Anchor, which is faid to have firft fuggefted to HANDEL the idea of bringing Oratorios on the ftage. And in 1732, *Efther* was performed at the Haymarket, Ten Nights. In March, 1733, *Deborah* was firft given to the public; and in April *Efther* was again exhibited at the fame theatre. It was during thefe early performances of Oratorios, that HANDEL firft gratified the public by the performance of CONCERTOS ON THE ORGAN, a fpecies of Mufic wholly of his own invention *(a)*, in which he ufually introduced an extempore fugue, a diapafon-piece, or an adagio, manifefting not only the wonderful fertility and readinefs of his invention, but the moft perfect accuracy and neatnefs of execution *(b)*.

It was in the fummer of 1733, that he went to the univerfity of Oxford, on occafion of a public act, taking with him Careftini, Strada, and his opera band: at this folemnity he had the Oratorio of *Athalia* performed in the public theatre, where he opened the organ in fuch a manner as aftonifhed every hearer. The late Mr. Michael Chriftian Fefting, and Dr. Arne, who were prefent, both affured me, that neither themfelves, nor any one elfe of their acquaintance, had ever before heard fuch extempore, or fuch premeditated playing, on that or any other inftrument.

In the Lent of 1734, he performed *Efther*, *Deborah*, and *Athalia*, at Covent-Garden; and in 1735, *Efther*, *Acis and Galatea*, and *Alexander's Feaft*, for the firft time. In 1738, *Ifrael*

(a) Rameau's *Livre de Pieces de Clavecin en Concerts*, did not appear till 1741.

(b) The favourite movement, at the end of his fecond organ-concerto, was long called the *Minuet in the Oratorio of Efther*, from the circumftance of its having been firft heard in the concerto which he played between the parts of that Oratorio.

in

in Egypt, and 1739, *Allegro ed il Penseroso.* During thefe laft
two years the Opera-houfe was fhut, and HANDEL's affairs were
at this time fo deranged, that he was under conftant apprehen-
fions of being arrefted by Del Pò, the hufband of Strada. This
ftimulated his friends to perfuade him to have a benefit; and, in
following their advice, he received fuch teftimonies of public favour at the Opera-houfe, in the Haymarket, March 28, 1738,
as proved extremely lucrative : for, befides every ufual part of the
houfe being uncommonly crouded, when the curtain drew up,
five hundred perfons of rank and fafhion were difcovered on the
ftage, which was formed into an amphitheatre *(a).*

In 1740, the Oratorio of *Saul* was performed, for the firft time,
at the theatre in Lincoln-Inn-Fields; and from this period,
HANDEL may be faid to have devoted his labours folely to the
fervice of the church; as, except his *grand Concertos for Violins,*
and the *Fire-work Mufic,* for the Peace of Aix la Chapelle, 1748;
I remember no other compofitions than Oratorios, that were ei-
either performed or publifhed by him *(b).*

During the firft years of his retreat from the Opera ftage, the
profits arifing from the performance of Oratorios were not fufficient to indemnify his loffes; and it would remain a perpetual

(a) This performance was called an *Oratorio*; but in examining the printed book of the words, with which I have been favoured by Mr. Belcher, one of HAN-DEL's few furviving friends, it appears that this exhibition was mifcellaneous; confift-ing of a mixture of facred and prophane, of Englifh and Italian Airs and Recitatives, without the leaft connection either in the words or mufic.

(b) From 1740, when he totally quit-ted the Opera-ftage, to 1751, he produced fifteen original Oratorios, and adapted Eng-lifh words to the mufic of a ferenata, or morality, *Il Trionfo del Tempo,* (the Triumph of Time and Truth) which he had fet to Ita-lian words, at Rome, 1709. Of thefe, the *Meffiah, Samfon,* and *Judas Macchabæus,* were fure to fill the houfe whenever they were performed; but though the reft are hazardous, and fluctuating in favour, yet there is no one of them which an exquifite and darling finger, fuch as Mrs. Sherridan, or Mrs. Bates, could not render important and attractive.

ftigma

ftigma on the tafte of the nation, if it fhould be recorded, that his MESSIAH, that truly noble and fublime work, was not only ill-attended, but ill-received, on its firft performance in 1741, were its mifcarriage not to be wholly afcribed to the refentment of the many great perfonages whom he had offended, in refufing to compofe for Senefino, by whom he thought himfelf affronted; or even for the Opera, unlefs that finger were difmiffed; which inflexibility being conftrued into infolence, was the caufe of powerful oppofitions that were at once oppreffive and mortifying.

HANDEL had been fo unfortunate in all his attempts to carry on Operas at the three feveral theatres of the Haymarket, Lincoln's-Inn-Fields, and Covent-Garden, in oppofition to his former protectors, the members of the Royal Academy, that he was reduced to the neceffity of drawing out of the funds ten thoufand pounds, which he had lodged there in his more profperous days; and ftill Strada, Montagnana, and other fingers employed in his laft Operas were unpaid, and obliged to quit this country with promiffory notes inftead of cafh.

HANDEL, however, who was a man of ftrict probity, and accuftomed to pay his performers not only honeftly, but generoufly, difcharged thefe debts very honourably, as foon as he was able.

It was after thefe repeated mifcarriages, and a very fevere illnefs, fuppofed to have been brought on by the joint effects of anxiety, mortification, diftrefs, and difappointment, that he went to Ireland, in order to try whether his Oratorios would be out of the reach of prejudice and enmity in that kingdom. Pope, on this occafion perfonifying the Italian Opera, put into her mouth the following well-known lines, which fhe addreffes to the goddefs of Dulnefs.

E   Strong

" Strong in new arms, lo! Giant HANDEL ſtands,
" Like bold Briareus, with his hundred hands;
" To ſtir, to rouſe, to ſhake the ſoul he comes,
" And Jove's own thunders follow Mars's drums.
" Arreſt him, empreſs; or you ſleep no more—
" She heard ;—and drove him to the Hibernian ſhóre *(a)*."

On his arrival at Dublin, with equal judgment and humanity, he began by performing the Meſſiah, for the benefit of the city priſon. This act of generoſity and benevolence met with univerſal approbation, as well as his Muſic; which, after ſpending ſome time in the diſcipline of his troops, was admirably performed, with Dubourg for leader, and the late Mrs. Cibber, to ſing, " *He was deſpiſed and rejected of Men.*" This air, the firſt, perhaps, in our language, has been often ſung by Italian ſingers of the greateſt abilities, but never, I believe, in a manner ſo truly touching to an Engliſhman, as by Mrs. Cibber, for whom it was originally compoſed; and whoſe voice, though a mere thread,

(a) When HANDEL went through Cheſter, in his way to Ireland, this year, 1741, I was at the Public-School in that city, and very well remember ſeeing him ſmoke a pipe, over a diſh of coffee, at the Exchange-Coffee-houſe; for being extremely curious to ſee ſo extraordinary a man, I watched him narrowly as long as he remained in Cheſter; which, on account of the wind being unfavourable for his embarking at Parkgate, was ſeveral days. During this time, he applied to Mr. Baker, the Organiſt, my firſt muſic-maſter, to know whether there were any choirmen in the cathedral who could ſing *at ſight*; as he wiſhed to prove ſome books that had been haſtily tranſcribed, by trying the choruſes which he intended to perform in Ireland. Mr. Baker mentioned ſome of the moſt likely ſingers then in Cheſter, and, among the reſt, a printer of the name of Janſon,

who had a good baſe voice, and was one of the beſt muſicians in the choir. At this time Harry Alcock, a good player, was the firſt violin at Cheſter, which was then a very muſical place; for beſides public performances, Mr. Prebendary Preſcott had a weekly concert, at which he was able to muſter eighteen or twenty performers, gentlemen, and profeſſors. A time was fixed for this private rehearſal at the *Golden Falcon*, where HANDEL was quartered; but, alas! on trial of the chorus in the Meſſiah, " *And with his ſtripes we are healed,*"— Poor Janſon, after repeated attempts, failed ſo egregiouſly, that HANDEL let looſe his great bear upon him; and after ſwearing in four or five languages, cried out in broken Engliſh: " You ſhcauntrel! tit not you dell me " dat you could ſing at ſoite?"—" Yes, " ſir, ſays the printer, and ſo I can; but " not at *firſt ſight.*"

and

and knowledge of Mufic, inconfiderable; yet, by a natural pathos, and perfect conception of the words, fhe often penetrated the heart, when others, with infinitely greater voice and fkill, could only reach the ear *(a)*.

HANDEL remained eight or nine months in Ireland, where he extended his fame, and began to repair his fortune. At his return to London, in the beginning of 1742, as he had relinquifhed all thoughts of oppofing the prefent managers of the Opera, former enmities began to fubfide; and, when he recommenced his Oratorios at Covent-Garden, the Lent following, he found a general difpofition in the public to countenance and fupport him. *Samfon* was the firft he performed this year, which was not only much applauded by crouded houfes in the capital, but was foon diffeminated, in fingle fongs, throughout the kingdom; and, indeed, it has ever been in the higheft favour of all his Oratorios, except the MESSIAH, which this feafon, to the honour of the public at large, and difgrace of cabal and faction, was received with univerfal admiration and applaufe. And from that time to the prefent, this great work has been heard in all parts of the kingdom with increafing reverence and delight; it has fed the hungry, clothed the naked, foftered the orphan, and enriched fucceeding managers of Oratorios, more than any fingle mufical production in this or any country.

This *Sacred Oratorio*, as it was at firft called, on account of the words being wholly compofed of genuine texts of Scripture, ap-

---

(a) One night, while HANDEL was in Dublin, Dubourg having a folo part in a fong, and a clofe to make, *ad libitum*, he wandered about in different keys a great while, and feemed indeed a little bewildered, and uncertain of his original key ... but, at length, coming to the fhake, which was to terminate this long clofe, HANDEL, to the great delight of the audience, and augmentation of applaufe, cried out loud enough to be heard in the moft remote parts of the theatre: " You are welcome home, Mr. Dubourg !"

E 2
pearing

pearing to ſtand in ſuch high eſtimation with the public, HAN-
DEL, actuated by motives of the pureſt benevolence and humanity, formed the laudable reſolution of performing it annually for
the benefit of the Foundling Hoſpital, which reſolution was conſtantly put in practice, to the end of his life, under his own direction ; and, long after, under that of Mr. Smith, and Mr. Stan-
ley. In conſequence of theſe performances, the benefactions to
the charity from the year 1749 to 1759, by eleven performances
under HANDEL's own direction, amounted to   -   £.6935 0 0

From 1760 to 1768, by eight performances under

    the conduct of Mr. John Chriſtian Smith   -   1332 0 0

From 1769 to 1777, nine performances under that

    that of Mr. Stanley   -   -   -   2032 0 0

                            £.10,299 0 0

The organ in the chapel of this hoſpital was likewiſe a preſent
from HANDEL; and he bequeathed, as a legacy to this charity,
a fair copy of the original ſcore of the MESSIAH.

From the time of his quitting Ireland, with little oppoſition,
and a few thin houſes, in conſequence of great aſſemblies of the
nobility and gentry, manifeſtly and cruelly collected together on his
nights of performance, with hoſtile intentions, by ſome implacable
remains of his moſt powerful adverſaries, he continued his Oratorios till within a week of his death (a).

But though the Oratorio of the MESSIAH increaſed in reputation every year, after his return from Ireland, and the crouds that

---

(a) The laſt ſeaſon of HANDEL's perſonal attendance and of his life was remarkably ſuccefsful. One of my friends, who was
generally at the performance of each Oratorio that year, and who uſed to viſit him
after it was over, in the treaſurer of the

theatre's office, ſays, that the money he
uſed to take to his carriage of a night, though
in gold and ſilver, was as likely to weigh
him down and throw him into a fever, as
the copper-money of the painter Coreggio,
if he had had as far to carry it.

                                     flocked

flocked to the theatre were more confiderable every time it was performed; yet, to fome of his other Oratorios, the houfes were fo thin, as not nearly to defray his expences; which, as he always employed a very numerous band, and paid his performers liberally, fo deranged his affairs, that in the year 1745, after two perform-ances of *Hercules*, January 5th and 12th, before the Lent feafon, he ftopped payment. He, however, refumed the performance of his Oratorios of *Samfon, Saul, Jofeph, Belfhazzar*, and the *Meffiah*, in March; but I perfectly remember, that none were well attended, except *Samfon*, and the MESSIAH *(a)*.

His late majefty king George the Second, was a fteady patron of HANDEL during thefe times, and conftantly attended his Oratorios, when they were abandoned by the reft of his court *(b)*.

HANDEL, late in life, like the great poets, Homer, and Mil-ton, was afflicted with blindnefs; which, however it might dif-pirit and embarrafs him at other times, had no effect on his nerves or intellects, in public: as he continued to play concertos and voluntaries between the parts of his Oratorios to the laft, with the fame vigour of thought and touch, for which he was ever fo juftly renowned. To fee him, however, led to the organ,

(a) In 1749, *Theodora* was fo very unfor-tunately abandoned, that he was glad if any profeffors, who did not perform, would ac-cept of tickets or orders for admiffion. Two gentlemen of that defcription, now living, having applied to HANDEL, after the dif-grace of *Theodora*, for an order to hear the MESSIAH, he cried out, "Oh your far-" vant, Mien-herren! you are tamnaple " tainty! you would not co to TEODORA— " der was room enough to tance dere, when " dat was perform."

Sometimes, however, I have heard him, as pleafantly as philofophically, confole hi friends, when, previous to the curtain being drawn up, they have lamented that the houfe was fo empty, by faying, "Nevre " moind; de moofic vil found de petter."

(b) About this time a *bon mot* of lord Chefterfield's was handed about by a noble-man, ftill living, who going one night to the Oratorio at Covent-Garden, met his lordfhip coming out of the theatre. "What! my lord, are you difmiffed? Is " there no Oratorio to-night?" "Yes, fays " his lordfhip, they are now performing; " but I thought it beft to retire, left " I fhould difturb the king in his *pri-* " *vacies*."

after

after this calamity, at upwards of feventy years of age, and then conducted towards the audience to make his accuftomed obeifance, was a fight fo truly afflicting and deplorable to perfons of fenfibility, as greatly diminifhed their pleafure, in hearing him perform.

During the Oratorio feafon, I have been told, that he practifed almoft inceffantly; and, indeed, that muft have been the cafe, or his memory uncommonly retentive; for, after his blindnefs, he played feveral of his *old* organ-concertos, which muft have been previoufly impreffed on his memory by practice. At laft, however, he rather chofe to truft to his inventive powers, than thofe of reminifcence: for, giving the band only the fkeleton, or ritornels of each movement, he played all the folo parts extempore, while the other inftruments left him, *ad libitum*; waiting for the fignal of a fhake, before they played fuch fragments of fymphony as they found in their books.

Indeed, he not only continued to perform in public after he was afflicted with blindnefs, but to *compofe* in private; for I have been affured, that the Duet and Chorus in *Judas Macchabæus*, of " *Sion now his head fhall raife, Tune your harps to fongs of* " *praife*," were dictated to Mr. Smith, by HANDEL, after the total privation of fight. This compofition, fo late in life, and under fuch depreffing circumftances, confirms an opinion of Dr. Johnfon, " that it feldom happens to men of powerful intellects " and original genius, to be robbed of mental vigour, by age; it " is only the feeble-minded and *fool-born* part of the creation, who " fall into that fpecies of imbecility, which gives occafion to fay " that they are *fuperannuated:* for thefe, when they retire late in " life from the world on which they have lived by retailing the " fenfe of others, are inftantly reduced to indigence of mind."

Dry-

Dryden, Newton, Dr. Johnſon himſelf, and our great Muſician, are admirable illuſtrations of this doctrine. Indeed, HANDEL not only exhibited great intellectual ability in the compoſition of this Duet and Chorus, but manifeſted his power of invention in extemporaneous flights of fancy to be as rich and rapid, a week before his deceaſe, as they had been for many years.   He was always much diſturbed and agitated by the ſimilar circumſtances of *Samſon*, whenever the affecting air in that Oratorio of " *Total Eclipſe, no Sun, no Moon,*" &c. was performed.

The laſt Oratorio at which he attended, and performed, was on the 6th of April, and he expired on *Friday* the 13th, 1759, and *not on Saturday the* 14*th*, as was at firſt erroneouſly engraved on his Monument, and recorded in his Life ; I have indiſputable authority for the contrary : as Dr. Warren, who attended HANDEL in his laſt ſickneſs, not only remembers his dying before midnight, on the 13th, but, that he was ſenſible of his approaching diſſolution ; and having been always impreſſed with a profound reverence for the doctrines and duties of the Chriſtian religion, that he had moſt ſeriouſly and devoutly wiſhed, for ſeveral days before his death, that he might breathe his laſt on *Good-Friday*, " in hopes, he ſaid, of meeting his " Good God, his ſweet Lord and Saviour, on the day of his reſur- " rection," meaning the third day, or the Eaſter Sunday following.

The figure of HANDEL was large, and he was ſomewhat corpulent, and unwieldy in his motions ; but his countenance, which I remember as perfectly as that of any man I ſaw but yeſterday, was full of fire and dignity ; and ſuch as impreſſed ideas of ſuperiority and genius.   He was impetuous, rough, and peremptory in his manners and converſation, but totally devoid of illnature or malevolence ; indeed, there was an original humour and pleaſantry in his moſt lively ſallies of anger or impatience, which,

with

with his broken English, were extremely rifible. His natural propenfity to wit and humour, and happy manner of relating common occurrences, in an uncommon way, enabled him to throw
perfons and things into very ridiculous attitudes. Had he been
as great a mafter of the Englifh language as Swift, his *bons mots*
would have been as frequent, and fomewhat of the fame kind.

HANDEL, with many virtues, was addicted to no vice that
was injurious to fociety. Nature, indeed, required a great fupply of fuftenance to fupport fo huge a mafs, and he was rather
epicurean in the choice of it; but this feems to have been the
only appetite he allowed himfelf to gratify *(a)*.

When

(a) The late Mr. Brown, leader of his majefty's band, ufed to tell me feveral ftories of HANDEL's love of good cheer, liquid and folid, as well as of his impatience. Of the former he gave an inftance, which was accidentally difcovered at his own houfe in Brook-ftreet, where Brown, in the Oratorio feafon, among other principal performers, was at dinner. During the repaft, HANDEL often cried out—" Oh—I " have de taught;" when the company, unwilling that, out of civility to them, the public fhould be robbed of any thing fo valuable as his mufical ideas, begged he would retire and write them down; with which requeft, however, he fo frequently complied, that, at laft, one of the moft fufpicious had the ill-bred curiofity to peep through the keyhole into the adjoining room; where he perceived that *defe taughts*, were only beftowed on a frefh hamper of *Burgundy*, which, as was afterwards difcovered, he had received in a prefent from his friend, the late lord Radnor, while his company was regaled with more generous and *fpirited* port.

Another anecdote which I had from Brown, was the following: When the late reverend Mr. Felton found that his firft organ concertos were well received, he opened a fubfcription for a fecond fet, and begged of Brown to folicit Mr. HANDEL's permiffion to infert his name in the lift. Brown, who had been in great favour with HANDEL the winter before, when he led his Oratorios, remembering how civilly he had been attended by him to the door, and how carefully cautioned, after being heated by a crouded room and hard labour, at the rehearfals in Brook-ftreet, not to ftir without a chair, had no doubt of his fuccefs: but, upon mentioning to him Felton's requeft, as delicately as poffible, one morning when he was fhaving, by telling him that he was a clergyman, who being about to publifh fome Concertos by fubfcription, was extremely ambitious of the honour of his name and acceptance of a book, merely to grace his lift, without involving him in any kind of expence; HANDEL, putting the barber's hand afide, got up in a fury, and, with his face ftill in a lather, cries out with great vehemence: " Tamn your feluf, and go to der " teiffel—a barfon make Concerto! why " he no make farmon?" &c. In fhort, Brown feeing him in fuch a rage, with razors in his reach, got out of the room as

faft

When Pope found that his friends, lord Burlington and Dr. Arbuthnot, thought fo highly of HANDEL, he not only lafhed his enemies in the Dunciad, but wifhed to have his *Eurydice* fet to Mufic by him. Mr. Belchier, a common friend, undertook to negotiate the bufinefs: but HANDEL having heard that Pope had made his Ode more lyrical, that is, fitter for Mufic, by dividing it into airs and recitatives, for Dr. Green, who had already fet it; and whom, as a partizan for Bononcini, and confederate with his enemies, he had long difliked, fays, "It is de very ding vat my *pellows-plower* "has fet already for ein tocktor's tecree at Cambridge *(a)*."

When Gluck came firft into England, in 1745, he was neither fo great a compofer, nor fo high in reputation, as he afterwards mounted; and I remember when Mrs. Cibber, in my hearing, afked HANDEL what fort of a compofer he was; his anfwer, prefaced by an oath---was, "he knows no more of contrapunto, "as mein cook, Waltz."

But though he was fo rough in his language, and in the habit of fwearing, a vice then much more in fafhion than at prefent,

faft as he could; left he fhould have ufed them in a more *barbarous* way than would be fafe. Indeed, he had a thorough contempt for all our compofers at this time, from Dr. Green down to Harry Burgefs; and performers on the organ too: for, after being long an inhabitant of this country, he ufed to fay, "When I came hither "firft, I found, among the Englifh, many "good players, and no compofers; but "now, they are all compofers, and no "players."

(a) Dr. Green took his degree at that univerfity in 1730. Indeed, on HANDEL's firft arrival in England, from Green's great admiration of this mafter's manner of playing, he had fometimes literally condefcended to become his *bellows-blower*, when he went to St. Paul's to play on that organ, for the exercife it afforded him, in the ufe of the pedals. HANDEL, after the three o'clock prayers, ufed frequently to get himfelf and young Green locked up in the church, together; and, in fummer, often ftript into his fhirt, and played till eight or nine o'clock at night. Dr. Green, previous to his admiffion into St. Paul's, as a chorifter, was taught to fing by the late Mr. Charles King; he was afterwards bound apprentice to Brind, the organift of that cathedral, and was, at the time alluded to by HANDEL, either ftill an apprentice, or, at leaft, a very young man, and deputy to the organift, whom he afterwards fucceeded.

F

he

he was truly pious, during the laſt years of his life, and conſtantly attended public prayers, twice a day, winter and ſummer, both in London and Tunbridge.

At the coronation of his late majeſty, George the Second, in 1727, HANDEL had words ſent to him, by the biſhops, for the anthems ; at which he murmured, and took offence, as he thought it implied his ignorance of the Holy Scriptures : " I have read " my Bible very well, and ſhall chuſe for myſelf." And, in- deed, his ſelection of the words, " *My heart is inditing of a good* " *matter*," was very judicious, and inſpired him with ſome of the fineſt thoughts that are to be found in all his works. This anthem was ſung at the coronation, while the peers were doing homage.

He knew the value of time too well to ſpend it in frivolous purſuits, or with futile companions, however high in rank. Fond of his art, and diligent in its cultivation, and the exerciſe of it, as a profeſſion, he ſpent ſo ſtudious and ſedentary a life, as ſeldom allowed him to mix in ſociety, or partake of public amuſements. Indeed, after my firſt arrival in London, 1744, he ſeldom was abſent from the benefit for Decayed Muſicians and their Families ; and I have ſometimes ſeen him at the Playhouſes, the Opera, and at St. Martin's church, when the late Mr. Kelway played the or- gan. But thoſe who were more intimately acquainted with him than myſelf, ſay, that in his latter years, except when he went to pay his duty to the royal family at St. James's, or Leiceſter-Houſe, he ſeldom viſited the great, or was viſible, but at church, and the performance of his own Oratorios.

Beſides ſeeing HANDEL, myſelf, at his own houſe, in Brook-ſtreet, and at Carlton-Houſe, where he had rehearſals of his Oratorios, by meeting him at Mrs. Cibber's, and, at Fraſi's, who was then my ſcholar, I acquired conſiderable knowledge of his private character,

and

and turn for humour. He was very fond of Mrs. Cibber, whose voice and manners had softened his severity for her want of musical knowledge. At her house, of a Sunday evening, he used to meet Quin, who, in spite of native roughness, was very fond of Music. Yet the first time Mrs. Cibber prevailed on HANDEL to sit down to the harpsichord, while he was present, on which occasion I remember the great Musician played the overture in *Siroe*, and delighted us all with the marvellous neatness with which he played the jig, at the end of it.—Quin, after HANDEL was gone, being asked by Mrs. Cibber, whether he did not think Mr. HANDEL had a charming hand? replied—" *a hand*, madam! you mistake, it's a *foot*,"— " Poh! poh! says she, has he not a fine finger?" " *Toes*, by G—, madam!"—Indeed, his hand was then so fat, that the knuckles, which usually appear convex, were like those of a child, dinted or dimpled in, so as to be rendered concave; however, his touch was so smooth, and the tone of the instrument so much cherished, that his fingers seemed to grow to the keys. They were so curved and compact, when he played, that no motion, and scarcely the fingers themselves, could be discovered.

At Frasi's, I remember, in the year 1748, he brought, in his pocket, the duet of *Judas Macchabæus*, " *From these dread* " *Scenes*," in which she had not sung when that Oratorio was first performed, in 1746. At the time he sat down to the harpsichord, to give her and me the time of it, while he sung her part, I hummed, at sight, the second, over his shoulder; in which he encouraged me, by desiring that I would sing out— but, unfortunately, something went wrong, and HANDEL, with his usual impetuosity, grew violent: a circumstance very terrific to a young musician.—At length, however, recovering from my fright, I ventured to say, that I fancied there was a mistake in the writing; which, upon examining, HANDEL discovered to be the

case:

cafe: and then, inftantly, with the greateft good humour and humility, faid, " I pec your barton—I am a very odd tog :— " maifhter Schmitt is to plame."

When Frafi told him, that fhe fhould ftudy hard, and was going to learn Thorough-Bafe, in order to accompany herfelf: HANDEL, who well knew how little this pleafing finger was addiêted to application and diligence, fays, " Oh—vaat may we " not expeêt !"

HANDEL wore an enormous white wig, and, when things went well at the Oratorio, it had a certain nod, or vibration, which manifefted his pleafure and fatisfaêtion. Without it, nice ob- fervers were certain that he was out of humour.

At the clofe of an air, the voice with which he ufed to cry out, CHORUS ! was extremely formidable indeed ; and, at the rehear- fals of his Oratorios, at Carleton-Houfe, if the prince and prin- cefs of Wales were not exaêt in coming into the Mufic-Room, he ufed to be very violent ; yet, fuch was the reverence with which his Royal Highnefs treated him, that, admitting HANDEL to have had caufe of complaint, he has been heard to fay, " Indeed, " it is cruel to have kept thefe poor people, meaning the per- " formers, fo long from their fcholars, and other concerns." But if the maids of honour, or any other female attendants, talked, during the performance, I fear that our modern Timotheus, not only fwore, but called names ; yet, at fuch times, the princefs of Wales, with her accuftomed mildnefs and benignity, ufed to fay, " Hufh ! hufh ! HANDEL's in a paffion."

HANDEL was in the habit of talking to himfelf, fo loud, that it was eafy for perfons not very near him, to hear the fubjeêt of his foliloquies. He had, by much perfuafion, received under his roof and proteêtion, a boy, who had been reprefented, not only as having an uncommon difpofition for mufic, but for fobriety and

diligence :

diligence: this boy, however, turned out ill, and ran away, no one, for a confiderable time, knew whither. During this period, HANDEL walking in the Park, as he thought, alone, was heard to commune with himfelf in the following manner.—" Der tei- " fel! de fater vas defheeved;—de mutter vas defheeved;—but " I vas not defheeved;—he is ein t—d fhcauntrel—and coot for " nutting."

HANDEL's general look was fomewhat heavy and four; but when he *did* fmile, it was his fire the fun, burfting out of a black cloud. There was a fudden flafh of intelligence, wit, and good humour, beaming in his countenance, which I hardly ever faw in any other.

It has been faid of him, that, out of his profeffion, he was ignorant and dull; but though I do not admit the fact, yet, if the charge were as true as it is fevere, it muft be allowed, in ex- tenuation, that to poffefs a difficult art in the perfect manner he did, and to be poffeffed by it, feems a natural confequence; and all that the public had a right to expect, as he pretended to no- thing more. Accomplifhments can only amufe our private friends, and ourfelves, in leifure hours; but fo occupied and abforbed was HANDEL, by the ftudy and exercife of his profeffion, that he had little time to beftow, either on private amufements, or the culti- vation of friendfhip. Indeed, the credit and reverence arifing from thefe, had HANDEL poffeffed them, would have been tran- fient, and confined to his own age and acquaintance; whereas the fame acquired by filent and clofe application to his profef- fional bufinefs,

——Nec Jovis ira, nec ignes,
Nec poterit ferrum, nec edax abolere vetuftas.

And

And it is probable, that his name, like that of many of his brethren, will long furvive his works. The moft learned man can
give us no information concerning either the private life or compofitions of Orpheus, Amphion, Linus, Olympus, Terpander,
or Timotheus, yet every fchool-boy can tell us, that they were
great Muficians, the delight of their feveral ages, and, many years
after, of pofterity.

Though totally free from the fordid vices of meannefs and ava-
rice, and poffeffed of their oppofite virtues, charity and genero-
fity, in fpite of temporary adverfity, powerful enemies, and frequent maladies of body, which fometimes extended to intellect,
HANDEL died worth upwards of Twenty Thoufand Pounds ;
which, except One Thoufand to the Fund for decayed Muficians
and their Families, he chiefly bequeathed to his relations on the
continent.

His funeral was not public, like that of Rameau, in France ;
of Jomelli, in Italy ; or of our Dryden, and Garrick, in England ;
yet, when he was buried in Weftminfter-Abbey, April the 20th,
1759, the dean, Dr. Pearce, bifhop of Rochefter, affifted by the
choir, performed the funeral folemnity. More general and national teftimonies of regard were left to the prefent period, when
all enmities, jealoufies, and operations of envy were fubfided ;
and when time, examination, and reflexion, had given new charms
and importance to his works. And this pleafing tafk has been
performed in a way fo ample, magnificent, and honourable, that
it will be difficult to find, either in ancient or modern hiftory, a
more liberal and fplendid example of gratitude to a deceafed artift,
in any other country.

CHARACTER of HANDEL as a COMPOSER.

THAT HANDEL was superior in the strength and boldness of his style, the richness of his harmony, and complication of parts, to every composer who has been most admired for such excellencies, cannot be disputed. And, while *fugue, contrivance*, and a *full score*, were more generally reverenced than at present, he remained wholly unrivalled.

I know it has been said that HANDEL was not the original and immediate inventor of several species of Music, for which his name has been celebrated; but, with respect to ORIGINALITY, it is a term to which proper limits should be set, before it is applied to the productions of any artist. Every *invention* is clumsy in its beginning, and Shakspeare was not the first writer of *Plays*, or Corelli the first composer of *violin Solos, Sonatas,* and *Concertos,* though those which he produced are the best of his time; nor was Milton the inventor of *Epic Poetry.* The scale, harmony, and cadence of Music, being settled, it is impossible for any composer to invent a GENUS of composition that is *wholly and rigorously new*, any more than for a poet to form a *language, idiom, and phraseology*, for himself. All that the greatest and boldest musical inventor *can* do, is to avail himself of the best effusions, combinations, and effects, of his predecessors; to arrange and apply them in a new manner; and to add, from his own source, whatever he can draw, that is grand, graceful, gay, pathetic, or, in any other way, pleasing. This HANDEL did, in a most ample and superior manner; being possessed, in his middle age and full vigour, of every refinement and perfection of his time: uniting the depth and elaborate contrivance of his own country, with Italian ele-

G

gance

gance and facility; as he feems, while he refided fouth of the Alps, to have liftened attentively in the church, theatre, and chamber, to the moft exquifite compofitions and performers, of every kind, that were then exifting.

And though we had CANTATAS by Cariffimi, Aleffandro Scarlatti, Gafparini, and Marcello; DUETS by Steffani and Clari; VOCAL CHORUSES, without inftrumental accompaniments, by Paleftrina, and our own Tallis, Bird, and Purcell; and, with accompaniments, by Cariffimi, as well as Paolo Colonna; with VIOLIN SONATAS and CONCERTOS by Corelli and Geminiani; yet it may with the utmoft truth be afferted, that HANDEL added confiderable beauties to whatever ftyle or fpecies of compofition he adopted, which, in a larger work, it would not be difficult to demonftrate, by examples. At prefent, I fhall only venture to give it as part of my mufical *profeffion de foi*, that his *air* or *melody* is greatly fuperior to any that can be found in the otherwife charming Cantatas which Cariffimi feems to have invented; that he is more natural in his voice-parts, and has given more *movement to his bafes* than Alef. Scarlatti; that he has more *force* and *originality* than Gafparini or Marcello; that his *chamber duets* are, at leaft, equal to thofe of Steffani and Clari, who were remarkable for no other fpecies of compofition; and though the late Dr. Boyce ufed to fay that HANDEL had great obligations to Colonna for his CHORUSES *with inftrumental accompaniments*, it feems indifputable that fuch chorufes were infinitely more obliged to HANDEL than he to Colonna, or, indeed, than they were to all the Compofers that have ever exifted. It is my belief, likewife, that the beft of his *Italian Opera Songs* furpafs, in variety of ftyle and ingenuity of accompaniment, thofe of all preceding and cotemporary Compofers throughout Europe; that he has more *fire*,

in

in his compofitions for violins, than Corelli, and more *rhythm* than Geminiani; that in his full, mafterly, and excellent *organ-fugues*, upon the moft natural and pleafing fubjects, he has furpaffed Frefcobaldi, and even Sebaftian Bach, and others of his countrymen, the moft renowned for abilities in this difficult and elaborate fpecies of compofition; and, laftly, that all the judicious and unprejudiced Muficians of every country, upon hearing or perufing his noble, majeftic, and frequently fublime FULL ANTHEMS, and ORATORIO CHORUSES, muft allow, with readinefs and rapture, that they are utterly unacquainted with any thing equal to them, among the works of the greateft mafters that have exifted fince the invention of counterpoint.

CHRO-

CHRONOLOGICAL LIST

OF

HANDEL'S WORKS.

ORIGINAL MANUSCRIPTS in the Poffeffion of his MAJESTY:

Amounting to Eighty-two Volumes.

OPERAS.

RODRIGO, performed at Florence	1709
AGRIPPINA - Venice	1709
RADAMISTO - London	1720
MUZIO SCEVOLA ——	1721
OTTONE - - ——	1722
GIULIO CESARE FLORIDANTE } ——	1723
FLAVIO	
TAMERLANO ——	1724
RODELINDA - ——	1725
ALESSANDRO } SCIPIONE ——	1726
RICARDO PRIMO ——	1727
TOLOMEO } SIROE ——	1728
LOTARIO - London	1729
PARTENOPE - ——	1730

PORO - - ——	1731
ORLANDO } SOSARME ——	1732
ARIANNA } EZIO - ——	1733
ARIODANTE - ——	1734
ALCINA - ——	1735
ARMINIO ATALANTA } GIUSTINO ——	1736
BERENICE } FARAMONDO ——	1737
SERSE - ——	1738
IMENEO } DEIDAMIA ——	1740

ORATORIOS.

ESTHER, compofed 1720, publickly performed in London 1732

DE-

DEBORAH — ⎫
ATHALIA   Oxford ⎬ 1733
TE DEUMS and JUBI-
LATE, 3 vols.

ACIS and GALATEA, at
Cannons, 1721, publick-
ly performed in London 1735

OPERA SONGS, 2 vols.
LAUDATE.
COLLECTION OF SONGS
AND CHORUSES.

ALEXANDER'S FEAST — 1735
ST. CECILIA'S ODE —— 1736
ISRAEL IN EGYPT —— 1738

MOTETTI è DUETTI.

L'ALLEGRO ED IL PEN-
SEROSO - - —— 1739

IL TRIONFO DEL ⎫ Rome 1709
TEMPO - ⎬ London 1737

SAUL - - —— 1740

ACIGE E GALA-
TEA - Napoli 1709

MESSIAH - —— 1741
SAMSON - —— 1742

ORATORIO ITALIANO.
CANTATE.

SEMELE -
BELSHAZZAR ⎫ —— 1743
SUSANNA ⎭

CONCERTI.
CONCERTI GROSSI.

HERCULES - —— 1744
OCCASIONAL ORATORIO
—— 1745

Tranfcript of VI SONA-
TAS for two Hautbois
and a Bafe - - 1694

JOSEPH - ⎫
JUDAS MACCHA- ⎬ —— 1746
BÆUS - ⎭

Not in HIS MAJESTY'S
Collection.

JOSHUA - ⎫
ALEXANDER BA- ⎬ —— 1747
LUS - - ⎭

ALMIRA, an Opera, per- ⎫
formed at Hamburgh ⎬ 1705
NERO - - - - —— ⎭

SOLOMON - —— 1749
THEODORA - London 1750
JEPHTHA - —— 1751

FLORINDO ⎫ —— 1708
DAFNE ⎭

RINALDO - London 1711

MISCELLANEOUS WORKS.
ANTHEMS, 8 vols.
CANTATAS, 4 vols.

TESEO - ⎫ —— 1712
PASTOR FIDO ⎭

AMADIGE - —— 1715
AMMETO - —— 1727

ALES-

ALESSANDRO SEVERO,

  PASTICCIO ——— 1737

PARNASSO IN FESTA

  -    -   ——— 1740

WATER-MUSIC ——— 1716

FIRE-WORK MUSIC——— 1748

TRIUMPH OF TIME AND

  TRUTH - ——— 1751

CHOICE OF HERCULES

  ——— 1745

SONATAS for two Violins

and a Bafe, two fets.

HARPSICHORD LESSONS,

  Two Books: the firft

  appeared in - 1720

FUGUES for the Organ.

ORGAN CONCERTOS,

  Three Sets.

CANTATAS, compofed at

  Hamburgh, between 1703

  and 1709

DITTO at Rome, 1709 and 1710

The late Mr. Walfh, of Catharine-ftreet, in the Strand, pur-chafed of HANDEL, for publication, tranfcripts of the Manu-fcript fcores of almoft all the works he had compofed in Eng-land; and Mr. Wright, of the fame place, fucceffor to Mr. Walfh, is ftill in poffeffion of thefe Manufcripts, many of which have never yet been publifhed. Little more than the favourite fongs of his Italian Operas, and thofe incorrectly, and in differ-ent forms, have, as yet, been printed. Of his Oratorios, befides the favourite Airs in all of them, Mr. Walfh's fucceffors have publifhed complete and uniform Scores of the MESSIAH, JU-DAS MACCHABÆUS, SAMSON, JEPHTHA, ISRAEL IN EGYPT, JOSHUA, SAUL, ESTHER, CHOICE OF HERCULES, L'ALLE-GRO ED IL PENSEROSO, DRYDEN'S ODE, ALEXANDER'S FEAST, ACIS AND GALATEA, BELSHAZZAR, SUSANNA, THE OCCASIONAL ORATORIO, and DEBORAH.

  Befides thefe, and his four CORONATION ANTHEMS, FU-NERAL ANTHEMS, GRAND TE DEUM, JUBILATE, and DETTINGEN TE DEUM, complete Scores of HANDEL'S TEN ANTHEMS, for voices and inftruments, compofed chiefly for the

duke

duke of Chandos, at Cannons, have been publifhed by Mr. Wright, in three volumes. The fame publifher is ftill in pof-feffion of many of his inedited Works: as Italian Duets, Can-tatas, Songs, Anthems, Sonatas, fome for violins, and fome for German flutes and a bafe, with feveral other mifcellaneous pro-ductions.

In the collection of the earl of Aylesford, formed by the late Mr. Jennings; and in that of Sir Watkin Williams Wynn, are preferved in MS. many valuable works of our author, as:

A CONCERTO for French Horns and Side Drum, with the March in JUDAS MACCHABÆUS.

Ditto for Trumpets and Horns.

Three CONCERTOS in Alexander's Feaft.

ORATORIO *della Paffione.*

Ditto *Della Refurrezione.*

TE DEUM, compofed on the Arrival of Queen Caroline.

Ditto in Bb for the Duke of Chandos.

Ditto in A, major 3^{d}.

DANCES in *Ariadne, Ariodante,* and *Paftor Fido.*

Several Harpfichord Leffons, not printed, fome of them for the Princefs Louifa.

Sir Watkin Williams Wynn, befides the printed OPERAS, ORATORIOS, and TE DEUMS, of HANDEL, is in poffeffion of the following Manufcript Scores: TE DEUM in A, and the ANTHEM, *Let God arife,* both tranfpofed and altered, for the King's Chapel.

I will magnify thee, compiled and altered, from feveral Anthems, for the Sons of the Clergy, at St. Paul's.

As pants the hart, for five voices; with feveral alterations and additions, by HANDEL himfelf, when it was introduced in the Oratorio of ESTHER.

The

The king shall rejoice. Performed at the Chapel-Royal, on the victory obtained at Dettingen.

Sing unto God. Performed at the nuptials of their late Royal Highnesses, the prince and princess of Wales, 1736.

Blessed are they: partly composed, and partly compiled, for the Foundling Hospital.

Let God arise, } Adapted to voices, without instruments,
As pants the hart. } for the Chapel Royal.

ODE, or SERENATA, composed for the birth-day of queen Anne.

And in the Collection of the late Barnard Granville, of Calwich, in Staffordshire, Esq. among 38 MS. folio volumes of HANDEL's works in Score, consisting of sixteen OPERAS, eleven ORATORIOS, 4 vols. of ANTHEMS, 1 of CANTATAS, others of TE DEUMS, CONCERTOS, and Miscellaneous Pieces, there are Scores of the Operas of RINALDO, TESEO, AMADIGE, and AMMETO, with 2 vols. of Duets, and one of Single Songs in Eight Parts.

———————

HIS MAJESTY, and the Directors of the CONCERT OF ANCIENT MUSIC, as well as many other admirers of the productions of HANDEL, having expressed a wish that a uniform and complete edition of all his various works, vocal and instrumental, might be engraved, in score; I shall give a place here to the following Proposals, which were published last year, and which every professor, as well as judge and lover of Music, must sincerely wish may be carried into execution, not only for the advancement of the art, but for the honour of this great Musician, and of our Country.

June

June 22, 1783.

HANDEL'S MUSIC.

P R O P O S A L S

For Printing by Subscription,

By R. BIRCHALL,

(From the late Mr. Randall's *Catherine-ftreet*)
Nº. 129, New Bond-Street.

COMPLETE SCORES of all the Compofitions of G. F. HANDEL, not hitherto perfected; Confifting of Italian Operas, Oratorios; a Number of Anthems, Te Deums, Cantatas and Trios (for Voices,) with other Miscellaneous Works; alfo his Instrumental Music, the whole of which is computed to make about Eighty Folio Volumes, containing one with another, near One Hundred and Fifty Pages each.

C O N D I T I O N S.

I. THE whole to be correctly engraved, and printed on Imperial Paper, to fuit fuch Oratorios and other Works, as are already printed complete.

II. An Elegant Engraving of the Author, to be given to the Subfcribers (only) in the courfe of the Work.

III. The Subfcription Price to be One Guinea a Volume, and, to non Subfcribers, One Guinea and a Half; the Subfcription Money to be paid on the Delivery of each Volume.

IV. The Subfcribers Names to be printed.

V. As foon as a fufficient Number is fubfcribed for, it is propofed to print a Volume every Month, till the whole is completed.

VI. That, as many Difappointments have happened to Publifhers of fuch Works, from Subfcribers changing the Places of their Abode, &c. and, as it would be imprudent, in the prefent Publifhers, to engage in this weighty Undertaking on an Uncertainty; it is humbly hoped, that fuch Noblemen, and Gentlemen, as wifh to encourage it, will authorize their Bankers, or Agents in London, to be anfwerable for the Subfcription Money, and to pay the fame, as above ftipulated, as well as to receive the Books.

Subscriptions received by BIRCHALL, at his Mufic-Shop, No. 129, NEW BOND-STREET, LONDON.

H

A D D E N D A

PREFACE OF THE COMMEMORATION ACCOUNT.

Page xi.

SINCE the Preface was printed, in which mention is made of the principal Mufical Performances of uncommon magnitude in other parts of Europe, anterior to the late Commemoration, I have been informed, that foon after my tour to Vienna, in 1772, a great Mufical Inftitution had been eftablifhed in that city for the Support of the Widows of deceafed Muficians, fomewhat refembling our Mufical Fund. As this eftablifhment has lately been mentioned in an anonymous book of Letters on the German Nation, written in the language of that country *(a)*, and is faid to have been productive of very extraordinary Mufical Exhibitions, both with refpect to the number of performers and accuracy of execution ; in order to obtain as authentic an account of them as poffible, I did myfelf the honour of waiting upon his Excellency Count Kageneck, the Imperial Envoy extraordinary and Minifter plenipotentiary at our court, by whom, after a full explanation of the fubject of my enquiries, I was defired to write down my queftions, with a promife that they fhould be accurately anfwered by the Count's fecretary, M. Schild, who is not only a native of Vienna, but a good Compofer, and practical Mufician.

At the time I prefented this gentleman with my queries, in writing, I had likewife the advantage of converfing with him on the fubject of Mufical Eftablifhments at Vienna ; and was foon after favoured with ample anfwers to my queftions ; of which, the following is the fubftance *(b)*.

(*a*) Briefe eines Reifenden Franzofen über Deutfchland an Seinen Bruder zu Paris. 2 vols. 8vo. 1785.

(*b*) The queftions were written in French, and anfwered in that language.

That

" That the Performances for the Benefit of Muficians Widows
" at Vienna have been eftablifhed about twelve years.

" That they confift of a kind of *Concert Spirituel*, or *Oratorio*,
" executed in the great national theatre twice a year : in Advent
" and Lent, by about three hundred and feventy vocal and inftru-
" mental performers ; and if there is an overflow of company,
" which fometimes happens, the performance at each of thefe fea-
" fons is repeated. The compofitions chofen on thefe occafions are
" not always the fame ; but Oratorios by Haffe, Gluck, Haydn,
" Ditters, Starzer, Salieri, and others ; and fometimes by an-
" cient German mafters : as HANDEL, Bach, Graun, and Rolle.

" And that the fum raifed at thefe performances annually
" amounts to about £500. each time."

On St. *Cecilia's-Day*, there is likewife a grand Mufical Performance at St. Stephen's Cathedral, the Metropolitan Church,
at which, befides the performers on the Choir eftablifhment, all
the moft eminent foreigners, as well as natives in Vienna at the
time, are ambitious to affift. The great Mafs, or Choral Mufic,
is ufually of the compofition of the prefent Maeftro di Capella,
Hoffmann, or of Reuter, Caldara, or Fuchs. This performance, as well as that of the Vefpers, on the eve of St. Cecilia,
is lefs remarkable for the number of hands and voices, which
amount only to about a hundred, than for the excellence of
the compofition and talents of the feveral Muficians who exert
themfelves on the occafion ; and who, between the different parts
of the fervice, perform Concertos, with folo parts, to difplay
their powers on their feveral inftruments *(a)*.

(a) Further particulars of thefe Mufical lume of *the General Hiftory of Mufic,* by
Eftablifhments will be given in the laft vo- the author of this account.

ADDENDA to LIFE of HANDEL.

(Page 10, after the 3d Period.)

IN the year 1718, when there seem to have been no Operas in England, Nicolini having quitted this country, was engaged at Naples, where HANDEL's RINALDO was brought on the stage, under the direction of the celebrated Leo, then a young man.

P. 16, after Note *(a)*.

Mattheson, in his book called the *Triumphal Arch*, mentions a circumstance concerning HANDEL, which is but little known in England. He says, that " in 1717, he was at Hanover with " his Royal and Electoral Highness, afterwards king George the " Second, to whom he had been just appointed maestro di ca- " pella." And as no Operas or other compositions appear in the list of his works, between the Opera of *Amadige*, 1715, and *Radamisto*, 1720, his attendance at the court of Hanover will help to fill up that chasm. Mattheson, who seems to have kept an exact record of the chief musical transactions of his time, particularly those which concern his intercourse with HANDEL, tells us, that he received letters from him that were written at Hanover, in 1717, concerning his dedicating to him, and other great masters, a work of his own, called the *Orchestra*, Part II. and in 1719, other letters from London, on the same subject.

Mattheson, in his **Ehren Pforte**, p. 96, speaks likewise of an Opera, set by HANDEL called *Oriana*, and performed at Hamburgh, 1717; and of *Judith*, an Oratorio, 1732, of which no-

thing

thing is known in England. He likewise mentions, in the same work, a Composition *for Paffion-Week*, of which the words were written by Brockes of Hamburgh. He says it was composed by HANDEL in England, 1719, and sent to that city, by post, in a very small score; but gives it no other name than a *Paffione*.

Tradition has preserved so many anecdotes concerning the performance of HANDEL at Hamburgh, that many musical people there, who came into the world too late to hear him, think they have lived in vain, and his works have at all times been in the highest favour in that city, where he began his career; for, besides the Operas already mentioned, which he composed expressly for the theatre in Hamburgh, at the beginning of this century, before he visited Italy, his *Rinaldo* was performed there in 1715; *Oriana*, 1717; *Agrippina*, 1718; *Zenobia*, 1721; *Mutius Scævola*, and *Floridantes*, 1723; *Tamerlano, Giulio Cefare*, and *Ottone*, 1725; *Ricardo Primo*, 1729; *Ammeto*, 1730; *Cleofida*, or *Poro*, and *Judith*, an Oratorio, 1732; and, lastly, *Rodelinda*, 1734, were all sent to Hamburgh from other places, and performed there in the absence of the composer.

Though some of his later Operas were performed on that stage, in Italian, yet the four first were set and sung in the German language; and others, after being performed in Italian, in London, were translated, altered, and totally changed for the Hamburgh stage, according to circumstances. Upon the whole, it appears, that nineteen or twenty of his Dramatic works had been performed there before the year 1740, when the *Triumphal Arch* was published.

While Mattheson was collecting materials for this work, he applied to HANDEL himself for an account of his Life and productions, which he promised to furnish; but, says Mattheson, " I am sorry to say that it remains still to be done."

In

In 1745, *Le Sécretaire des Commandemens de sa Majesté Britannique*, as Mattheson sometimes styles himself, dedicated to HANDEL what he calls *the well-founding finger-language* (𝕯𝖎𝖊 𝖜𝖔𝖑=𝖐𝖑𝖎𝖓𝖌𝖊𝖓𝖉𝖊 𝖋𝖎𝖓𝖌𝖊𝖗=𝖋𝖕𝖗𝖆𝖈𝖍𝖊) by which he means a book of 12 fugues for the organ, on two and three subjects; and received from him the following letter.

      Monsieur,   *à Londres, ce 29 de Juillet, 1735.*

    IL y a quelque tems, que j'ai reçue une de vos obligeantes lettres; mais à présent je viens de recevoir votre derniere, avec votre ouvrage.

    Je vous en remercie, Monsieur, et je vous assure qui j'ai toute l'estime pour votre merite: je souhaiterois seulement, que mes circonstances m'étoient plus favorables, *pour vous donner des marques de mon inclination pour vous servir. L'ouvrage est digne de l'attention des connoisseurs, & quant à moi, je vous rend justice.*

    Au reste, pour rammasser quelque epoque, il m'est impossible, puisqu' une continuelle application au service de cette cour & noblesse me detourne de toute autre affaire.

    Je suis avec une consideration trés parfaite, &c.

    S I R,   London, July 29, 1735.

    IT is a considerable time since I received your first obliging letter; and now I am favoured with a second, accompanied by your work.

    I thank you for it, Sir; and assure you that I have a sincere esteem for your merit: I only wish *that I was in more favourable circumstances* for manifesting my inclination to serve you. The work is well worthy the attention of the curious; and for my own part, I am always ready to do you justice.

    As for drawing up memoirs concerning myself, I find it utterly impossible, on account of my being continually occupied in the service of the court and nobility, which puts it out of my power to think of any thing else.   I am with perfect regard, *&c.*

                                         " Since

" Since which time, fays Matthefon, till 1739, when the
" court and firft nobility, and, indeed, the whole nation, were
" more attentive to a ruinous war, than to places of public enter-
" tainment, this could be no excufe. I therefore repeated my
" requeft, inforced by all the arguments I could devife, but ftill
" to no purpofe."

In fpeaking of HANDEL's works at this time (1740),
Matthefon fays, " he compofed from his own knowledge and re-
" fources;" and fpeaks of feveral Anthems and choral compofitions, particularly of his *Grand Te Deum*, not knowing that it
was already printed. " His 8 *Pieces de Clavecin*, fays he, were
" engraved on copper in 1720, and fince that, a fecond fet,
" which are very fine; but to acquire the poffeffion of thefe and
" his other great works, I have been prevented by their high
" price. However, I feem, continues he, to have had fome
" claims upon a man to whom, in his feeble beginnings, I ma-
" nifefted much kindnefs, and afterwards fhewed him great refpect
" in the eulogiums I beftowed on him in my writings, as well as
" in dedicating my works to him, at no inconfiderable expence.
" And if he had thought *me* unworthy of fuch confidence, the
" mufical public, at leaft, who adored him, merited fuch a mark
" of refpect. We were early companions at the Opera, in our
" ftudies and performance, at the table, and in our rambles.
" *We took fweet counfel together, and walked in the houfe of God*
" *as friends.*"

Matthefon feems to have been very imperfectly acquainted with
the mufical tranfactions of England at this time, as well as of the
fituation of poor HANDEL's affairs; who, oppofed, perfecuted,
impoverifhed, and, by extreme agitation and anxiety, injured both
in health and intellects, was fo far from being able to patronize

his

his old acquaintance and competitor, that he ftood in great need of patronage himfelf; and indeed, he was, perhaps, ftill lefs able to undertake a retrofpect fcrutiny and examination of his own life and circumftances; for, being naturally proud, and neither ignorant of his own powers, nor infenfible to dignity of character, this was by no means a favourable time for felf-examination. It is chiefly in moments of profperity, happinefs, or vanity, that men can have much pleafure in thinking or talking about themfelves; and as HANDEL was unfortunate, unhappy, and " too ❧ proud to be vain," a requeft that he would become his own biographer was not likely to be granted.

Mattthefon, on the contrary, was fo far from having a repugnance to fuch a humiliating employment, that he not only furnifhed all the articles concerning himfelf that were printed in Walther, Marpurg, and other cotemporary mufical writers, but was continually blazoning his abilities and importance in his own works. The truth is, that his authority for the praife he beftows on others is never fufpected, as it is given unwillingly; fo that he ftill continues to be cited by his countrymen as an author of knowledge and veracity. And his tranflation and critical remarks on the Life of HANDEL are ftill referred to, as claffical.

However, Mattthefon, though he found himfelf the dupe of unreafonable expectation, concludes his account of him in his *Triumphal Arch*, by telling his countrymen that HANDEL had been offered a Doctor's degree in Mufic at the univerfity of Oxford, which he had declined; but that a marble ftatue had been erected to him in Vauxhall Gardens, an honour feldom conferred on living artifts in modern times; and concludes by faying, that " no one can praife our famous HANDEL more than I myfelf " have done, in my mufical writings; particularly in my *Mufica*
" *Critica,*

" *Critica*, 1722; *Mufical Patriot*, 1728; *Kernel of Melodious*
" *Science*, 1737; and *Perfect Chapel-Mafter*, 1739." Indeed,
there are no mufical writers in the German language whofe works
have come to my hands, that do not mention HANDEL with
great reverence.

Walther, in his Mufical Lexicon, 1732, ftyles him " a very
" celebrated maeftro di capella, then in England;" and gives a
lift of his Operas which had been performed at Hamburgh.

Quantz, the late celebrated mafter to the king of Pruffia on
the German flute, in his own Life, written by himfelf, fpeaking
of the ftate of Mufic in England when he was there, 1727, fays,
that the greateft performer then on the harpfichord and organ in
London, was HANDEL; on the violin, Geminiani; on the
hautbois, Martini; and on the flute, Weideman. HANDEL's orcheftra at the Opera, he fays, was uncommonly powerful; and
the bafes in his compofitions were fuperior to the trebles in thofe
of Bononcini.

Scheiben, in his *Critical Mufician*, publifhed at Leipfig, 1745,
fays, that though Kuhnau and Keifer were very great muficians,
they were obliged to give way to HANDEL and *Telemann*. HAN-
DEL, though he often worked upon his own materials, yet dif-
dained not to ufe the thoughts of others; particularly thofe of Rein-
hard Keifer. And in all his works he difcovered great intelligence in his art, and the utmoft purity of harmony, and fimplicity of melody.

Marpurg, in his Treatife on the Art of Fugue, 1756, calls
him a claffical Compofer, no lefs renowned for his Church-
Mufic, full of admirable fugues, than for his theatrical productions, beautiful overtures, organ fugues, harpfichord leffons, and
a moft fublime manner of playing the organ. This author, in his

I   Critical

Critical Letters on Mufic, Berlin, 1760, fpeaks of the fugue in the fecond Overture of *Admetus*, as a compofition that he can, never hear without emotion. Indeed, HANDEL has manifefted wonderful abilities in that fugue, by inverting a very curious and difficult fubject, in all the anfwers.

Hiller, of Leipfic, in his *Weekly Mufical Journal*, 1767, where he gives a lift of HANDEL's Operas performed in England, fpeaks of his genius and abilities with feeling and intelligence; and an idea may be formed of the veneration in which he is ftill held at Hamburgh, by the following particulars.

M. Schuback, fyndic of Hamburgh, a refpectable magiftrate and able mufician, has employed, according to his own account, all his leifure hours, during almoft forty years, in the ftudy and imitation of his great countryman, HANDEL *(a)*. And this ingenious *Amateur* has compofed, and publifhed an Oratorio, called *The Difciples at Emmaus*, profeffedly in the ftyle of HANDEL *(b)*.

(a) In 1779, I was honoured with a letter from M. Schuback, in which is inferted the following eloge of our favourite compofer : *Vous trouverez à ce que j'efpere, que je fuis imitateur, foible à la verité, mais zelé pourtant, du fameux* HANDEL. *Ce grand homme me paroit toujours le premier compofiteur qui fut jamais, et il y a près de 40 ans que je tache de fuivre fes traces; ce que je fcaurois prouver par une quantité d'ouvrages, trop grandes, je le confeffe, pour un homme qui étant employé aux fervices de l'état, n'a qu'à derober quelques heures, pour fatisfaire à l'envie dont il eft chatouillé de primer fur les maitres de chapelle.*——In another letter M. Schuback tells me, that in 1777, HANDEL's *Te Deum, Meffiah,* and *Alexander's Feaft*, were performed at Hamburgh, under his direction, for the benefit of the poor.

(b) This Oratorio may be had, in fcore, with German or Englifh words, of Mr. Napier, at his Mufic-fhop, in the Strand, N° 474. It was wholly compofed for tenor and bafe voices, on account of an irreconcileable quarrel, for precedence, which happened among the female fingers at Hamburgh, 1778.

COMMEMORATION

OF

HANDEL.

B

INTRODUCTION.

HOW this great idea was generated, cherished, and matured, will, probably, be a matter of curiosity to the public, as well as the manner in which it was executed. And having had the honour of attending many of the meetings of the
Directors and Conductor, while the necessary arrangements were
under consideration, as well as opportunities of conversing with
them, since, I shall state the principal facts as accurately as possible, from such authentic information as these favourable circumstances have furnished.

In a conversation between lord viscount Fitzwilliam, sir Watkin Williams Wynn, and Joah Bates, esquire, commissioner of
the Victualling-Office, the beginning of last year, 1783, at the
house of the latter, after remarking that the number of eminent
musical performers of all kinds, both vocal and instrumental,
with which London abounded, was far greater than in any other
city of Europe, it was lamented that there was no public pe-
riodical occasion for collecting and consolidating them into one
band; by which means a performance might be exhibited on so
grand and magnificent a scale as no other part of the world could
equal. The birth and death of HANDEL naturally occurred to
three such enthusiastic admirers of that great master, and it was

imme-

immediately recollected, that the next (now the prefent) year, would be a proper time for the introduction of fuch a cuftom : as it formed a *complete century* fince his birth, and an exact *quarter of a century* fince his deceafe.

The plan was foon after communicated to the governors of the Mufical Fund, who approved it, and promifed their affiftance. It was next fubmitted to the directors of the concert of Ancient Mufic, who, with an alacrity which does honour to their zeal for the memory of the great artift HANDEL, voluntarily under-took the trouble of managing and directing the celebrity. At length, the defign coming to the knowledge of the king, it was honoured with his Majefty's fanction and patronage. Weftminfter-Abbey, where the bones of the great mufician were depofited, was thought the propereft place for the performance ; and appli-cation having been made to the bifhop of Rochefter for the ufe of it, his lordfhip, finding that the fcheme was honoured with the patronage of his majefty, readily confented ; only requefting, as the performance would interfere with the annual benefit for the Weftminfter Infirmary, that part of the profits might be appro-priated to that charity, as an indemnification for the lofs it would fuftain. To this the projectors of the plan acceded ; and it was afterwards fettled, that the profits of the firft day's performance fhould be equally divided between the Mufical Fund and the Weftminfter Infirmary ; and thofe of the fubfequent days be *folely* applied to the ufe of that fund which HANDEL himfelf fo long helped to fuftain, and to which he not only bequeathed a thoufand pounds, but which almoft every Mufician in the capital annually contributes his money, his performance, or both, to fupport.

Application was next made to Mr. James Wyatt, the architect, to furnifh plans for the neceffary decorations of the abbey ; draw-ings

ings of which having been fhewn to his Majefty, were approved.
The general idea was to produce the effect of a royal mufical chapel, with the orcheftra terminating one end, and the accommo-
dations for the Royal Family, the other.

The arrangement of the performance of each day was next fettled, and I have authority to fay, that it was at his majefty's in-
ftigation that the celebrity was extended to three days inftead of
two, which he thought would not be fufficient for the difplay of
HANDEL's powers, or fulfilling the charitable purpofes to which
it was intended to devote the profits. It was originally intended
to have celebrated this grand Mufical Feftival on the 20th, 22d,
and 23d of April; and the 20th being the day of the funeral of
HANDEL, part of the Mufic was, in fome meafure, fo felected
as to apply to that incident. But, in confequence of the fudden
diffolution of parliament, it was thought proper to defer the feftival to the 26th, 27th, and 29th of May, which feems to have
been for its advantage: as many perfons of tender conftitutions,
who ventured to go to Weftminfter-Abbey in warm weather,
would not have had the courage to go thither in cold.

Impreffed with a reverence for the memory of HANDEL, no
fooner was the project known, but moft of the practical Muficians in the kingdom eagerly manifefted their zeal for the enterprife; and many of the moft eminent profeffors, waving all claims
to precedence in the band, offered to perform in any fubordinate
ftation, in which their talents could be moft ufeful.

By the latter end of February the plan and neceffary arrangements were fo far digefted and advanced, that the Directors ventured to infert in all the Newfpapers, the following advertife-
ment.

" Under

" Under the Patronage of His MAJESTY.
In Commemoration of HANDEL, who was buried in Weftminfter-
Abbey, on the 21ft of April, 1759.
On WEDNESDAY the 21ft of April next, will be performed in
Weftminfter-Abbey, under the management of the

Earl of Exeter	Lord Paget
Earl of Sandwich	Right Hon. H. Morrice
Vifcount Dudley Ward	Sir Watkin Williams Wynn, Bart.
Vifcount Fitzwilliam	Sir Richard Jebb, Bart.

Directors of the Concert of Ancient Mufic;

Some of the moft approved pieces of Sacred Mufic, of that great
Compofer.—The doors will be opened at Nine o'Clock, and the performance will begin precifely at Twelve.

And on the Evening of the fame day, will be performed, at the
Pantheon, a Grand Mifcellaneous CONCERT of Vocal and Inftrumental Mufic; confifting entirely of pieces felected from the works
of Handel.—The doors will be opened at Six o'Clock, and the Concert will begin exactly at Eight.

And on Saturday Morning, April 24th, will be performed, in Weftminfter Abbey, the Sacred Oratorio of the MESSIAH.

Such is the reverence for this illuftrious Mafter, that moft of the
performers in London, and a great many from different parts of the
kingdom, have generoufly offered their affiftance; and the Orcheftra
will confift of at leaft Four Hundred Performers, a more numerous
Band than was ever known to be collected in any country, or on any
occafion whatever. The profits arifing from the performances, will be
applied to charitable purpofes.

The Directors of the Concert of Antient Mufic have opened books
to receive the names of fuch perfons as are defirous of encouraging this
undertaking, and will deliver out the Tickets for the feveral performances, at ONE GUINEA each. Books will likewife be opened, and
Tickets delivered at Mr. Lee's, No. 44, Wigmore-ftreet; Birchell's
Mufic-fhop, No. 129, New Bond-ftreet; Longman and Broderip's, in
the Haymarket and Cheapfide; Bremner's, near the new Church in
the Strand; and at Wright's and Co. Catherine-ftreet, Strand.

No perfon will be admitted without a ticket; and it is hoped, that
thofe who mean to fubfcribe, will do it as early as they conveniently
can, that proper feats may be provided for them."

In

In order to render the band as powerful and complete as poſſible, it was determined to employ every ſpecies of inſtrument that was capable of producing grand effects in a great orcheſtra, and ſpacious building. Among theſe, the SACBUT, or DOUBLE TRUMPET, was ſought; but ſo many years had elapſed ſince it had been uſed in this kingdom, that, neither the inſtrument, nor a performer upon it, could eaſily be found. It was, however, diſcovered, after much uſeleſs enquiry, not only here, but by letter, on the continent, that in his Majeſty's military band there were ſix muſicians who played the three ſeveral ſpecies of ſacbut; tenor, baſe, and double baſe *(a)*. The names of theſe performers will be found in the general liſt of the band.

The DOUBLE BASSOON, which was ſo conſpicuous in the Orcheſtra and powerful in its effect, is likewiſe a tube of ſixteen feet. It was made with the approbation of Mr. HANDEL, by Stainſby, the Flute-maker, for the coronation of his late majeſty, George the Second. The late ingenious Mr. Lampe, author of the juſtly admired Muſic of *the Dragon of Wantley*, was the perſon intended to perform on it; but, for want of a proper reed, or for ſome other cauſe, at preſent unknown, no uſe was made of it, at that time; nor, indeed, though it has been often attempted, was it ever introduced into any band in England, till now, by the ingenuity and perſeverance of Mr. Aſhly, of the Guards.

THE DOUBLE-BASE KETTLE DRUMS were made from models of Mr. Aſbridge, of Drury-lane orcheſtra, in

(a) The moſt common ſacbut, which the Italians call *trombone*, and the Germans *Poſaune*, is an octave below the common trumpet; its length eight feet, when folded, and ſixteen, ſtrait. There is a manual, by which a note can be acquired a fourth lower than the uſual loweſt ſound on the trumpet, and all the tones and ſemitones of the common ſcale.

copper,

copper, it being impoffible to procure plates of brafs, large enough. The Tower-drums, which by permiffion of his grace the duke of Richmond, were brought to the Abbey on this oc-cafion, are thofe which belong to the Ordnance ftores, and were taken by the duke of Marlborough at the battle of Malplaquet, in 1709. Thefe are hemifpherical, or a circle divided ; but thofe of Mr. Afbridge are more cylindrical, being much longer, as well as more capacious, than the common kettle-drum ; by which he ac-counts for the fuperiority of their tone to that of all other drums. Thefe three fpecies of kettle-drums, which may be called tenor, bafe, and double-bafe, were an octave below each other.

The excellent ORGAN, erected at the weft end of the Abbey, for the commemoration performances only, is the workmanfhip of the ingenious Mr. Samuel Green, of Iflington. It was fabri-cated for the cathedral of Canterbury, but before its departure for the place of its deftination, it was permitted to be opened in the capital on this memorable occafion. The keys of communication with the harpfichord, at which Mr. Bates, the conductor, was feated, extended nineteen feet from the body of the organ, and twenty feet feven inches below the perpendicular of the fet of keys by which it is ufually played. Similar keys were firft con-trived in this country for HANDEL himfelf, at his Oratorios ; but to convey them to fo great a diftance from the inftrument, with-out rendering the touch impracticably heavy, required uncommon ingenuity and mechanical refources.

In celebrating the difpofition, difcipline, and effects, of this moft numerous and excellent band, the merit of the admirable architect who furnifhed the elegant defigns for the Orcheftra and Galleries, muft not be forgotten ; as, when filled, they confti-tuted one of the grandeft and moft magnificent fpectacles which

imagi-

imagination can delineate. I am acquainted with few buildings, that have been conftructed from plans of Mr. Wyatt, in which he exercifed his genius in *Gothic*; but all the preparations for receiving their Majefties, and the firft perfonages in the kingdom, at the eaft end; upwards of Five Hundred Muficians at the weft; and the public in general, to the number of between three and four thoufand perfons, in the area and galleries, fo wonderfully correfponded with the ftyle of architecture of this venerable and beautiful ftructure, that there was nothing vifible, either for ufe or ornament, which did not harmonize with the principal tone of the building, and which may not, metaphorically, have been faid to be in *perfect tune* with it. But, befides the wonderful manner in which this conftruction exhibited the band to the fpectators, the Orcheftra was fo judicioufly contrived, that almoft every performer, both vocal and inftrumental, was in full view of the conductor and leader; which accounts, in fome meafure, for the uncommon eafe with which the performers confefs they executed their parts.

The whole preparations for thefe grand performances were comprifed within the weftern part of the building, or broad aifle; and fome excellent judges declared, that, apart from their beauty, they never had feen fo wonderful a piece of carpentry, as the Orcheftra and Galleries, after Mr. Wyatt's models. Indeed, the goodnefs of the workmanfhip was demonftrated by the whole four days of commemoration in the Abbey being exempted from every fpecies of accident, notwithftanding the great crouds, and conflicts for places, which each performance produced.

At the eaft end of the aifle, juft before the back of the choir-organ, fome of the pipes of which were vifible below, a throne was erected in a beautiful Gothic ftyle, correfponding with that of the Abbey, and a center box, richly decorated and furnifhed

C   with

with crimfon fatin, fringed with gold, for the reception of their Majefties and the Royal Family; on the right hand of which was a box for the Bifhops, and, on the left, one for the Dean and Chapter of Weftminfter; immediately below thefe two boxes were two others, one, on the right, for the families and friends of the Directors, and the other for thofe of the prebendaries of Weft-minfter. Immediately below the King's-box was placed one for the Directors themfelves; who were all diftinguifhed by white wands tipped with gold, and gold medals, ftruck on the occafion, appending from white ribbands. Thefe their Majefties likewife condefcended to wear, at each performance. Behind, and on each fide of the throne, there were feats for their Majefty's fuite, maids of honour, grooms of the bedchamber, pages, &c.

The Orcheftra was built at the oppofite extremity, afcending regularly from the height of feven feet from the floor, to upwards of forty, from the bafe of the pillars; and extending from the centre to the top of the fide aifle.

The intermediate fpace below was filled up with level benches, and appropriated to the early fubfcribers. The fide aifles were formed into long galleries, ranging with the Orcheftra, and af-cending, fo as to contain twelve rows on each fide: the fronts of which projected before the pillars, and were ornamented with feftoons of crimfon morine.

At the top of the Orcheftra was placed the occafional organ, in a Gothic frame, mounting to, and mingling with, the faints and martyrs reprefented in the painted glafs on the weft window. On each fide of the organ, clofe to the window, were placed the kettle-drums, defcribed above. The choral bands were princi-pally placed in view of Mr. Bates, on fteps, feemingly afcending into the clouds, in each of the fide aifles, as their termination

was

was invifible to the audience. The principal fingers were ranged in the front of the Orcheftra, as at Oratorios, accompanied by the choirs of St. Paul, the Abbey, Windfor, and the Chapel-Royal.

The defign of appointing *Subdirectors*, was to diminifh, as much as poffible, the trouble of the noblemen and gentlemen who had projected the undertaking, as well as that of the Conductor : and this was effected with great diligence and zeal, not only in fuper-intending the bufinefs at the doors of admiffion, and conducting the company to their feats, which fell to the fhare of Dr. Cook, Dr. Ayrton, and meffieurs Jones, Aylward, and Parfons, all profeffors of the firft clafs ; but in arranging the performers, and conveying fignals to the feveral parts of that wide-extended Orcheftra : departments which fell to the lot of Dr. Arnold and Mr. Dupuis, organifts and compofers to his Majefty, and Mr. Redmond Simpfon, eminent and refpectable profeffors, of great experience, who may be faid to have acted as *Adjutant-Generals* on the occafion ; Dr. Arnold and Mr. Depuis having been placed, on different fides of the Orcheftra, over the vocal choir, and Mr. Simpfon in the centre, over the fubordinate inftrumental performers. In felecting thefe delegates among the members of the Mufical Society, great care was taken not to enfeeble the Orcheftra, by employing fuch performers as were likely to augment its force ; but fuch as had either ceafed to play in public, or whofe inftruments being the organ and harpfichord, of which only one was wanted, accepted of parts which were not the lefs ufeful for being *filently* performed.

Of the care and intelligence with which preparations were made for thefe performances, fome judgment may be formed from the fingle circumftance of the Mufic-books that were provided for

each

each day : as two hundred and feventy-four were requifite for the firft performance, in the Abbey; a hundred and thirty-eight for the Pantheon ; and two hundred and fixty-feven for the Meffiah ; amounting, in all, to feven hundred and feventy-nine ; not one of which was miffing, or miflaid, nor was an inftrument wanting during the whole commemoration : as the porters had ftrict orders to convey all the inftruments into the orcheftra, at the Abbey, by feven o'clock in the morning of each day, to prevent the company from being incommoded by the admiffion of fuch as were unwieldy.

Few circumftances will, perhaps, more aftonifh veteran Muficians, than to be informed, that there was but *one general Rehearfal* for each day's performance : an indifputable proof of the high ftate of cultivation to which practical Mufic is at prefent arrived in this country; for, if good performers had not been found, ready made, a *dozen* rehearfals would not have been fufficient to make them fo. Indeed, Mr. Bates, in examining the lift of performers, and enquiring into their feveral merits, fuggefted the idea of what he called a *drilling Rehearfal,* at Tottenham-ftreet Concert-Room, a week before the performance ; in order to hear fuch volunteers, particularly chorus-fingers, as were but little known to himfelf, or of whofe abilities his affiftant was unable to fpeak with certainty *(a).* At this rehearfal, though it confifted of a hundred and twenty performers, not more than two of that number were defired to attend no more.

At the general rehearfal in the Abbey, mentioned above, more than five hundred perfons found means to obtain admiffion, in

(a) This was Mr. John Afhly, of the Guards, whofe unwearied zeal and diligence were conftantly employed with fuch intelligence and fuccefs, as greatly facilitated the advancement of the plan, and diminifhed the anxiety of Mr. Bates, as well as the weight with which he had voluntarily loaded his fhoulders.

fpite

ſpite of every endeavour to ſhut out all but the performers; for fear of interruption, and, perhaps, of failure in the firſt attempts at incorporating and conſolidating ſuch a numerous band: conſiſting, not only of all the regulars, both native and foreign, which the capital could furniſh, but all the irregulars, that is, *dilettanti*, and provincial Muſicians of character, who could be muſtered, many of whom had never heard or ſeen each other before. This intruſion, which was very much to the diſſatisfaction of the Managers and Conductor, ſuggeſted the idea of turning the eagerneſs of the public to ſome profitable account for the charity, by fixing the price of admiſſion to Half a Guinea for each perſon.

But, beſides the profits derived from ſubſequent rehearſals, the conſequences of the firſt were not without their uſe: for the pleaſure and aſtoniſhment of the audience, at the ſmall miſtakes, and great effects of this firſt experiment, which many had condemned by anticipation, were ſoon communicated to the lovers of Muſic, throughout the town, to the great increaſe of ſubſcribers and ſolicitors for tickets. For though the friends of the Directors were early in ſubſcribing, perhaps, from perſonal reſpect, as much as expectation of a higher muſical repaſt than uſual; yet, the public, in general, did not manifeſt great eagerneſs in ſecuring tickets, till after this rehearſal, Friday, May 21, which was reported to have aſtoniſhed even the performers themſelves, by its correctneſs and effects. But ſo intereſting did the undertaking become, by this favourable rumour, that from the great demand of tickets, it was found neceſſary to cloſe the ſubſcription; which was done ſo rigorouſly, that the author of this account was unable, on Monday, to obtain of the Managers tickets of any kind, on any terms, for ſome of his friends, who had neglected to give in their names ſooner.

Many

Many families, as well as individuals, were, however, attracted to the capital by this celebrity; and I never remember it so full, not only so late in the year, but at any time in my life, except at the coronation of his present Majesty. Many of the performers came, unsolicited, from the remotest parts of the kingdom, at their own expence; some of them, however, were afterwards reimbursed, and had a small gratuity in consideration of the time they were kept from their families, by the two unexpected additional performances.

Foreigners, particularly the French, must be much astonished at so numerous a band moving in such exact measure, without the assistance of a *Coryphæus* to beat the time, either with a roll of paper, or a noisy *baton*, or truncheon. Rousseau says, that " the " more time is beaten, the less it is kept;" and, it is certain, that when the measure is broken, the fury of the musical-general, or director, increasing with the disobedience and confusion of his troops, he becomes more violent, and his strokes and gesticulations more ridiculous, in proportion to their disorder.

The celebrated Lulli, whose favour in France, during the last century, was equal to that of HANDEL in England, during the present, may be said to have *beat himself to death*, by intemperate passion in marking the measure to an ill-disciplined band; for in regulating, with his cane, the time of a *Te Deum*, which he had composed for the recovery of his royal patron, Louis XIV. from a dangerous sickness, in 1686, he wounded his foot by accidentally striking on that instead of the floor, in so violent a manner, that, from the contusion occasioned by the blow, a mortification ensued, which cost him his life, at the age of fifty-four!

As this Commemoration is not only the first instance of a band of such magnitude being assembled together, but of *any*

band,

band, at all numerous, performing in a fimilar fituation, without the affiftance of a *Manu-ductor*, to regulate the meafure, the
performances in Weftminfter-Abbey may be fafely pronounced,
no lefs remarkable for the multiplicity of voices and inftruments
employed, than for accuracy and precifion. When all the wheels
of that huge machine, the Orcheftra, were in motion, the effect
refembled clock-work in every thing, but want of feeling and expreffion.

And, as the power of gravity and attraction in bodies is proportioned to their mafs and denfity, fo it feems as if the magnitude of
this band had commanded and impelled adhefion and obedience,
beyond that of any other of inferior force.   The pulfations in every
limb, and ramifications of veins and arteries in an animal, could
not be more reciprocal, ifochronous, and under the regulation of
the heart, than the members of this body of Muficians under that
of the Conductor and Leader.   The totality of found feemed to
proceed from one voice, and one inftrument ; and its powers produced, not only new and exquifite fenfations in judges and lovers
of the art, but were felt by thofe who never received pleafure
from Mufic before.

Thefe effects, which will be long remembered by the prefent
public, perhaps to the difadvantage of all other choral performances, run the rifk of being doubted by all but thofe who heard
them, and the prefent defcription of being pronounced fabulous,
if it fhould furvive the prefent generation.

ASSISTANT DIRECTORS.

Dr. Benjamin Cooke,
Dr. Samuel Arnold,
Dr. Edmund Ayrton,
Mr. Redmond Simpson,

Mr. Thomas Saunders Dupuis,
Mr. John Jones,
Mr. Theodore Aylward,
Mr. William Parsons.

ASSISTANT CONDUCTOR,
Mr. John Ashley.

INSTRUMENTAL PERFORMERS.

ORGAN.
JOAH BATES, Esquire.

FIRST VIOLINS.
PRINCIPALS.

Mr. Hay
Mr. Cramer

Rev. Mr. Attwood
Mr. Agus
Mr. Barret
Mr. Barron
Mr. Baffet
Mr. Bishop
Mr. Blake
Mr. Boultflower
Mr. Brooks
Mr. Cabanes
Mr. Chabran
Mr. Cole
Mr. Condel
Mr. Coyle
Mr. Coyle, jun. Organist,
    Ludlow, Shropshire
Mr. Crouch
Mr. Dance
Mr. Denby, Derby
Mr. Fifin

Mr. Fox
Mr. Frudd, Nottingham
Mr. Gillingham
Mr. Gwilliam
Mr. Hellendael
Mr. Hime
Mr. Hindmarsh
Mr. Howard
Mr. Henry
Mr. Hobbs
Mr. Huxtable
Mr. Johnstone
Mr. Lanzoni
Mr. J. Mahon, Oxford
Mr. Oliver
Mr. Parkinson
Mr. Salpietro
Mr. Robert Shaw
Mr. Anthony Shaw
Mr. G. Shutz
Mr. Thomas Smith
Mr. Thackary, York
Mr. Thurstan
Mr. Tibet
Mr. Wood

Mr. Wakefield
Mr. Watson

SECOND VIOLINS.
PRINCIPALS.

Mr. Borghi
Mr. Soderini

Master Ashley
Mr. Churchill
Mr. Coles
Mr. Compton
Mr. Crofs
Mr. Evans
Mr. Farlow
Mr. Fell
Mr. Foulis
Mr. French
Mr. Gallot
Mr. Gehot
Mr. Guisbach
Mr. Guisbach, jun.
Mr. Hackman
Mr. Higgins
Mr. Hodson

D   Mr.

Mr. Howlds
Mr. Jackfon
Mr. Inchbald
Mr. Linton
Mr. Long
Mr. Miller
Mr. Nicholfon
Mr. Norbon
Mr. J. Parkinfon
Mr. Peck
Mr. Pinto
Mr. Rawlins
Mr. Reinegale
Mr. T. Shaw
Mr. J. Smith
Mr. Robert Smith
Mr. Smithergale
Mr. Stanard
Mr. Stayner
Mr. Valentine, jun.
Mr. Vidini
Mr. Wagner
Mr. D. Walker
Mr. Ware, jun.
Mr. Warren
Mr. Watley
Mr. Williams
Mr. Woodcock

TENORS.
PRINCIPALS.

Mr. Napier
Mr. Carnevale
Mr. Hackwood
Mr. Shields

Mr. Benfer
Mr. Buckinger
Rev. Mr. Flye
Mr. Gibbons
Mr. Jackfon
Mr. G. Jones
Mr. W. Mahon
Mr. Mefling
Mr. Miller
Mr. Pick
Mr. J. Richards
Mr. Rock
Mr. Sharp, jun. Grant-
ham, Lincolnfhire

Mr. Sharp, St. Neott's
Huntingdonfhire
Mr. D. Shaw
Mr. Simpfon
Mr. Turner
Mr. Valentine, Leicefter
Mr. Vial
Mr. Villenieu
Mr. Warren, fen.
Mr. Wilcock

HAUTBOIS.
PRINCIPALS.

Mr. Vincent
Mr. Fifcher
Mr. Eiffert
Mr. Parke

Mr. Brandi
Mr. Cantelo
Mr. Fofter
Mr. Kneller
Mr. Munro
Mr. Parke, jun.
Mr. Partri
Mr. F. Sharp, Grantham,
Lincolnfhire
Mr. Suck

2d HAUTBOIS.

Mr. Arnult
Mr. Coles
Mr. Cornifh
Mr. Dickenfon
Mr. Gray
Mr. Heinitz
Mr. Karift
Mr. Leffler, jun.
Mr. Lowe
Mr. Maniffire
Mr. Pope
Mr. Rice
Mr. Teed

FLUTES.

Mr. Buckley
Mr. Decamp

Mr. Florio
Mr. Huttley
Mr. Papendick
Mr. Potter

VIOLONCELLOS.
PRINCIPALS.

Mr. Crofdill
Mr. Cervetto
Mr. Paxton
Mr. Mara

Mr. Adams
Mr. Barron, jun.
Mr. Beilby
Mr. Bradford
Mr. Denny
Mr. Guifbach
Mr. Hill
Mr. Mafon
Mr. Mawby
Mr. Phillips
Mr. Roberts
Mr. Scola
Mr. William Sharp
Mr John Shields
Mr. Sikes
Mr. J. Smith
Mr. Zeidler

BASSOONS.
PRINCIPALS.

Mr. Baumgarten
Mr. Hogg
Mr. Lion
Mr. Parkinfon

Mr. Bodwin
Mr. Browning
Mr. Denman
Mr. Evans
Mr. Gough
Mr. Holmes
Mr. Hubbard
Mr. Jenkinfon
Mr. King
Mr. Kneller

Mr.

Mr. Leffler
Mr. Lings
Mr. Mallet
Mr. Ofborn
Mr. Peacocke
Mr. Pondsford
Mr. Schubert
Mr. R. Shaw
Mr. Ralph Shaw
Mr. Windfor
Mr. J. Windfor
Mr. Zink

DOUBLE BASSOON.
Mr. Afhley

DOUBLE BASSES.
PRINCIPALS.
Mr. Gariboldi
Mr. Richard Sharp
Mr. Neibour
Mr. Pafquali

Mr. Barret
Mr. Drefsler
Mr. Granthony
Mr. B. Hill
Mr. J. Hill

Mr. King
Mr. Kirton
Mr. Philpot
Mr. J. Sharp
Mr. Smart
Mr. Thompfon

TRUMPETS.
PRINCIPALS.
Mr. Sarjant
Mr. Jenkins
Mr. Vinicomb
Mr. Fitzgerald

Mr. Atwood
Mr. Cantelo
Mr. Flack
Mr. W. Jones
Mr. Marley
Mr. Nicola
Mr. Porney
Mr. Tompfon

TROMBONI, or SACBUTS.
Mr. Karft
Mr. Kneller
Mr. Moeller
Mr. Neibour

Mr. Pick
Mr. Zink.
Thefe performers played on other inftruments, when the facbuts were not wanted.

HORNS.
Mr. Englifh
Mr. Gray
Mr. Kaye
Mr. Leander
Mr. Lely
Mr. Lord
Mr. M'Pherfon
Mr. Miller
Mr. Moeller
Mr. Ockle
Mr. Payola
Mr. Pieltin

KETTLE-DRUMS.
Mr. Burnet
Mr. Houghton
Mr. Nelfon

DOUBLE KETTLE-DRUM.
Mr. Afhbridge

VOCAL PERFORMERS.

TREBLES.
PRINCIPALS.
Madame Mara
Mifs Harwood
Mifs Cantelo
Mifs Abrams
Mifs T. Abrams
Signor Pacchierotti, at the Pantheon only
Signor Bartolini

Three Mafter Afhleys
Mifs Burnet

Mafter Bellamy
Mrs. Burnet
Ten Chapel Boys
Mafter Dorion
Mifs Hudfon
Two Mafter Knyvetts
Mafter Latter
Mafter Loader
Mrs. Love
Mafter Lowther
Mafter Mathews
Mifs Middleton
Mifs Parke

Ten St. Paul's Boys
Mafter Piper
Mafter Taylor
Eight Weftminfter Boys
Six Windfor Boys.

COUNTER TENORS.
PRINCIPALS.
Rev. Mr. Clerk
Mr. Dyne
Mr. Knyvett

Mr.

Baron Dillon
Mr. W. Ayrton, York-
  shire
Mr. Barrow
Mr. Battishall
Mr. Bowen
Mr. Bushby
Rev. Mr. Champnefs
Rev. Mr. Comins, Exeter
Mr. Dowding
Mr. Fawcett
Mr. Friend
Mr. Gore, Windsor
Mr. Green
Mr. Guichard
Mr. Geo. Harris
Mr. Hartly, Windsor
Mr. Harwood, Lancashire
Mr. Hindle
Mr. Horsfall
Mr. Leach
Mr. Lewis
Mr. Livefque
Mr. Ivitt Loulworth, Cam-
  bridgeshire
Mr. Machin
Mr. Moulds
Mr. Offield
Mr. Parker
Mr. Pemberton
Mr. Percy
Mr. Reinholdfon
Mr. Roberts
Mr. Rofe
Mr. Salmon, Worcefter
Mr. Slater
Mr. Smith
Mr. Starkey, Oxford
Mr. Steel
Mr. Stevenfon, Hunting-
  don
Mr. Swaine
Mr. Swan
M.. Taylor
Mr. Vincent
Mr. Walton, Litchfield
Rev. Mr. O. Wight
Mr. Wilfon

TENORS.

PRINCIPALS.

Mr. Harrifon
Mr. Norris, Oxford
Mr. Corfe, Salifbury

Mr. Abington
Mr. Arrowfmith
Mr. Atterbury, Tedding-
  ton, Middlefex.
Mr. Aylmer
Mr. Ayrton, jun.
Mr. Bacon
Mr. Tho. Baker
Mr. Bethal
Mr. Billington
Mr. Bloomer
Mr. Booth
Mr. Bond
Mr. Bryan
Mr. Burlington
Mr. Bufby
Mr. Cheefe, Manchefter
Mr. Chriftian
Mr. Ed. Clarke
Mr. William Clarke
Mr. Comins, Penzance,
  Cornwall
Mr. Matthew Cooke
Mr. Robert Cooke
Mr. Dale
Mr. Darvile
Mr. Darvile, jun.
Mr. Deeble
Mr. Degnum
Mr. Dorion
Mr. Evance
Mr. Evance, jun.
Mr. Field
Mr. Florio, jun.
Mr. Foulfton
Mr. Gillatt
Mr. Gilfon
Mr. Guife, Windsor
Mr. Heather
Mr. Hewitt
Mr. Hill, Salifbury
Mr. Hobler
Mr. Holcroft

Mr. Hudfon
Mr. Jackfon
Mr. Immyns
Mr. King, Stilton, Hunt-
  ingdonfhire
Mr. Keith
Mr. Latter
Mr. Lloyd
Mr. Luther
Mr. Malmes
Mr. Minchine
Mr. Noble, Peterborough
Mr. J. Ogden, near Man-
  chefter
Mr. Olive
Mr. Piercy
Mr. Pitt, Worcefter
Mr. Plumer
Mr. Probyn, Birmingham
Mr. William Rocke
Mr. Randal
Mr. Reeve
Mr. Remy
Mr. M. Roch
Mr. J. Roch
Mr. Sexton, Windfor
Mr. Squire
Mr. Stafford Smith
Mr. Stanton
Mr. Stevens
Mr. Taylor
Mr. Tett
Mr. J. Tett
Mr. Turtle
Mr. Vincent, jun.
Mr. Webb, jun.
Mr. White
Mr. Whitehead
Mr. Williams
Mr. Wilfon
Mr. Woodhead

BASSES.

PRINCIPALS.

Mr. Bellamy
Mr. Champnefs
Mr. Reinhold
Signor Tafca
Mr. Mathews, Oxford

Mr.

Mr. William Baker
Mr. Balmforth
Mr. Boyce
Mr. Brewſter
Mr. Briggs
Mr. Buckingham
Mr. Burton
Mr. Calcot
Mr. Clay
Mr. Crawley
Mr. Crippen
Mr. Coke
Mr. Culver
Mr. Danby
Mr. Danby, jun.
Mr. Darley
Mr. Duncomb
Mr. Fiſher
Rev. Mr. Gibbons
Mr. W. Granville
Mr. Greatorex, ſen. Burton upon Trent
Mr. Greatorex, jun. Newcaſtle
Mr. James Green
Mr. Thomas Green, Birmingham

Mr. Groombridge
Mr. Hargrave
Mr. Harris, Birmingham
Mr. Richard Harris
Mr. J. Harriſon, Derbyſhire
Mr. F. Hatfield
Mr. Henſhaw
Mr. Holden, Birmingham
Rev. Mr. Horner
Mr. Howard
Mr. Joyce
Mr. Langdon, Peterborough
Mr. Linton
Mr. Lockhart
Mr. Ludworth
Mr. Lynott
Rev. Dr. Morgan
Mr. Miller
Mr. Milton
Mr. Olive
Mr. Ofmand
Mr. Overend, Iſleworth
Mr. Pemberton
Mr. Price
Mr. Purcell
Mr. Rainbott,
Mr. Rawſon, Nottingham

Mr. Real
Mr. Robinſon, Windſor
Mr. Robſon, Huntingdonſhire
Mr. Roebuck
Mr. Rogers
Mr. Henry Roſe
Mr. Rutter, Windſor
Mr. Sales, jun. Windſor
Mr. Salter
Mr. Sands
Mr. Saunders
Mr. Slater, jun.
Mr. Smart
Mr. Smith, Richmond
Mr. John Swan
Mr. Joſeph Swan
Mr. Taylor
Mr. Benj. Thomas
Mr. John Thomas
Mr. Tombs, Wincheſter
Mr. Tomſon
Mr. Townſend
Mr. Waite
Mr. Watts
Mr. Webb
Mr. Wheatley, Greenwich
Mr. Wheatly, jun.
Rev. Mr. Willet

COM-

WESTMINSTER ABBEY
COMMEMORATION
OF HANDEL

MAY XXVI MDCCLXXXIV

COMMEMORATION

OF

HANDEL.

FIRST PERFORMANCE,

WESTMINSTER-ABBEY,

WEDNESDAY, May 26, 1784.

[To face P. 24.]

LIST of the Compositions selected from the Works of
HANDEL,

For the first Commemoration Performance.

The CORONATION ANTHEM.

PART I.

OVERTURE—ESTHER.
The Dettingen TE DEUM.

PART II.

OVERTURE, with the DEAD MARCH in SAUL.
Part of the FUNERAL ANTHEM.
When the ear heard him.
He delivered the poor that cried.
His body is buried in Peace.
GLORIA PATRI, from the JUBILATE.

PART III.

ANTHEM—*O sing unto the Lord.*
CHORUS—*The Lord shall reign*, from ISRAEL IN EGYPT.

Plan of the Orchestra, and Disposition of the Band.

First Bass Voices
First Bass Voices
First Bass Voices
First Bass Voices
First Tenor Voices
First Tenor Voices
First Tenor Voices
First Alto Voices
First Alto Voices
1st Alto Voices
1st Alto Voices

Oboes
Oboes
Pi. Oboes
Double Basses
Violoncellos

Trumpets
Trumpets
Trumpets
Trumpets
Trumpets

Double Drums. Drums. Tenor Drums.

Tenors
Tenors
Tenors
Tenors
1st Violins
1st Violins
1st Violins
1st Violins
1st Violins
1st Violins

2d Violins
2d Violins
2d Violins
2d Violins
2d Violins

Crown.

Tenors
Tenors
Cornos
Cornos
Cornos
Cornos

Trombone

P.1 Violin
Organ Keys
P.1 Violoncello
D. Bass
P.1 Violoncello
D. Bass
D. Bass

Mr Bates Esqr Conductor.

Dr Bassoon
Double Bass
Double Bass
Violoncello
Violoncello
P.1 Bassoon
2d Bassoon
2d Bassoon
Second Bassoon
1st Violins
2d Violins
2d Violins
2d Violins

First Canto Voices
First Canto Voices
1st Canto Voices
2d Canto
2d Canto
2d Canto Voices
Cantos Voices
2d Alto Voices
2d Alto Voices
2d Alto Voices
Second Alto Voices
Second Tenor Voices
Second Tenor Voices
Second Tenor Voices
Second Bass Voices
Second Bass Voices
Second Bass Voices
Second Bass Voices

Principal Singers

PART I.

EARLY in the morning, the weather being very favourable, perſons of all ranks quitted their carriages with impatience and apprehenſion, left they ſhould not obtain ſeats, and preſented themſelves at the ſeveral doors of Weſtminſter Abbey, which were advertiſed to be opened at Nine o'clock; but the door-keepers not having taken their poſts, and the Orcheſtra not being wholly finiſhed, or, perhaps, the reſt of the Abbey quite ready for the reception of the audience, till near Ten o'clock; ſuch a croud of ladies and gentlemen were aſſembled together as became very formidable and terrific to each other, particularly the female part of the expectants; for ſome of theſe being in full dreſs, and every inſtant more and more incommoded and alarmed, by the violence of thoſe who preſſed forward, in order to get near the door, ſcreamed; others fainted; and all were diſmayed and apprehenſive of fatal conſequences: as many of the moſt violent, among the gentlemen, threatened to break open the doors; a mea-ſure, which if adopted, would, probably, have coſt many of the moſt feeble and helpleſs their lives; as they muſt, infallibly, have been thrown down, and trampled on, by the robuſt and impatient part of the croud.

It was a conſiderable time after a ſmall door at the weſt end was opened, before this preſs abated: as tickets could not be

examined

examined, and cheques given in return, faft enough, to diminifh the candidates for admiffion, or their impatience.

However, except difhevelled hair, and torn garments, no real mifchief feems to have happened. In lefs than an hour after the doors were opened, the whole area and galleries of the Abbey feemed too full for the admiffion of more company ; and a confiderable time before the performance began, the doors were all fhut to every one but their Majefties, and their fuite, who arrived foon after Twelve ; and on entering the box, prepared for their reception, pleafure and aftonifhment, at the fight of the company and difpofition of the Orcheftra and Performers, were painted fo ftrongly in their countenances, as to be vifible to all their delighted fubjects prefent. Eagernefs and expectation for the *premier coup d'archet* were now wound up to the higheft pitch of impatience ; when a filence, the moft profound and folemn, was gently interrupted by the proceffional fymphony of the

CORONATION ANTHEM,
Compofed in 1727.

" *Zadoc the prieft, and Nathan the prophet, anointed Solomon*
" *king : and all the people rejoiced ; and faid, God fave the king :*
" *long live the king : may the king live for ever. Hallelujah.*
" *Amen.*"   1 Kings i. 38.

And from the time that the firft found of this celebrated, and well-known compofition, was heard, to the final clofe, every hearer feemed afraid of breathing, left it fhould obftruct the ftream of harmony in its paffage to the ear.

From the progrefs which practical Mufic has made in this country, fince HANDEL's time, it might, perhaps, be fafely pronounced,

nounced, that this Anthem was never fo well performed, under his own direction.   As I heard it myfelf at the Coronation of his prefent Majefty, when a numerous band was affembled under the direction of the late Doctor Boyce, I can, at leaft, venture to fay that, in recollection, the performance then will bear no comparifon with that now, in the fame place, in honour of the compofer *(a)*.

OVERTURE IN ESTHER,
Compofed in 1720.

The firft movement of this grave and majeftic Overture has always aftonifhed me, by the fimplicity of its modulation ; which, though almoft rigoroufly confined to the diatonic intervals, and harmony of the key, is never monotonous in its effects.   And the firft bar of the melody, though fo often repeated by the two violins, is fo grateful and pleafing, as to be always welcome to the ear.

All the movements of this admirable Overture firft appeared in HANDEL's *Trios,* as did many of thofe he introduced afterwards in his Organ Concertos ; and he might with more truth have faid of thofe Trios : *Condo et compono, quæ mox depromere poffim,* than Geminiani, of his laft, and worft fet of Concertos.

(a) There was, doubtlefs, the greateft propriety in faluting their Majefties, at their entrance, with the *Coronation Anthem* ; and yet, I could not help wifhing, that this performance, fo different from all others, had opened with fome piece in which every voice and every inftrument might have been heard at the fame inftant ; as fuch an effect might then have been produced, as can never be obtained by gradation : the difference between *nothing* and *fomething* being greater, than between any two degrees of excellence. Indeed, the moft fudden and *furprifing* effect of this ftupendous band, was, perhaps, produced by fimultaneous tuning : as all the ftringed-inftruments performed this tafk, *à double corde,* and thefe ftrings being all *open,* their force was more than equal to that of two ftopt-ftrings, upon two different inftruments.

The fecond movement, which has always been juftly admired for the gravity and contraft between the trebles, which frequently repeat a fragment of canto fermo, and the bafe, had a moft ftriking effect given to it, by the force and energy of this band. And the fugue, which is compofed upon a moft marked and happy fubject, though feldom in more than three parts, as the tenor conftantly plays an octave above the bafe, feemed more rich in harmony, and ingenious in contrivance, to-day, than ufual. There never was, perhaps, an inftrumental fugue on a more agreeable fubject; treated in a more mafterly manner; or more pleafing in its effects, than this; which differs in feveral circumftances from almoft all other fugues: firft, in the given fubject being accompanied by an airy moving bafe; fecondly, by the reverfion of the fubject, when firft anfwered by the fecond violin; and thirdly, by the epifodes, or folo parts, for the hautbois *(a)*. This overture, almoft ever fince it was compofed, has been fo conftantly played at Saint Paul's, at the Feaft of the Sons of the Clergy, that it now feems in a peculiar manner dedicated to the fervice of the Church.

THE DETTINGEN TE DEUM
Compofed in 1743.

This fplendid production has been fo frequently performed at Saint Paul's and elfewhere, that nothing could be added to its celebrity by my feeble praife. I fhall only obferve, that as it was compofed for a military triumph, the fourteen trumpets, two pair

(a) Thefe folo parts were played by twelve hautbois, in unifon; which united in fuch a manner, as to have the effect of a fingle inftrument. The fhort folo part for the hautbois in the flow movement, was performed, by Mr. Tho. Vincent, alone, who fo long enjoyed the favour of the town upon that inftrument.

of

of common kettle-drums, two pair of double drums from the Tower, and a pair of double-bafe drums, made exprefsly for this Commemoration, were introduced with great propriety; indeed, thefe laft drums, except the deftruction, had all the effect of the moft powerful artillery.

There is fome reafon to fufpect that HANDEL, in fetting his grand *Te Deum* for the peace of Utrecht, as well as this, confined the meaning of the word *cry* to a forrowful fenfe: as both the movements to the words———

" *To thee all angels* cry *aloud,*"

are not only in a minor-key, but flow, and plaintive. It contrafts well, however, with the preceding and fubfequent movements. Indeed, the latter glows with all the fire and vehemence of HANDEL's genius for polyphonic combinations and contrivances.

The grave and folemn praife of the *Apoftles*, *Prophets*, and *Martyrs*, meafured by the conftant majeftic motion of the bafe, is well fymbolized.

" *Thou fitteft at the right hand of God,*" &c.

is expreffed in a ftrain that is remarkably pleafing, and which, in fpite of forty years, ftill retains all the bloom and frefhnefs of novelty: and

" *We therefore pray thee help thy fervants, whom thou haft re-*
" *deemed with thy precious blood,*"

is admirable, in fugue, modulation, and counterpoint, *à Capella*; as is the next movement, to the three verfes:

" *Make them to be numbered——*
" *O Lord fave thy people—*and
" *Govern them and lift them up for ever,*"

with the additional merit of a happy verbal expreffion.

" *Day*

" *Day by day we magnify thee,*"

is grand and well accented, though some of the trumpet paſſages are a little *viellis*. The art of fugue, both in that, and the next verſe :

" *And we worſhip thy name ever world without end,*"

is treated with HANDEL's uſual clearneſs and felicity.

As he was ſure of a great and varied band, when he compoſed this *Te Deum,* he has made as judicious a uſe of the ſeveral inſtruments of his Orcheſtra, as a painter could do of the colours on his palette : now exhibiting them in their full luſtre, ſingly ; then augmenting or diminiſhing their force, by light and ſhade, and often by combination with others, making them ſubſervient to different purpoſes of expreſſion and effect.

" *Vouchſafe, O Lord, to keep us this day without ſin,*"

is ſet to an exquiſite ſtrain, in which the modulation is no leſs ſurpriſing, learned, and curious, than pathetic and pleaſing *(a)*.

The laſt movement :

O Lord, in thee have I truſted—&c."

is what the Italians would allow to be *ben tirato*. Indeed, it is an excellent diſplay of HANDEL's reſources in diſcovering and availing himſelf of the moſt latent advantages which every ſimple as well as artificial ſubject affords him. The ſymphony of this Chorus, which is chiefly conſtructed upon a *ground-baſe*, beginning by two trumpets, that are afterwards joined by the other inſtruments, is ſtately and intereſting, though in the meaſure of a

(a) The ſcore of this movement, as printed many years ſince, by Walſh, is extremely incorrect ; particularly in the ſecond violin and tenor parts of the laſt line, bars four and five.

common

common minuet. The long folo part, after the fymphony, for a contralto voice, with foft and fparing accompaniments, renders the fubfequent fudden burft of all the voices and inftruments the more ftriking. And the latter part, in fugue, with an alternate ufe of the ground-bafe, feems to wind up this magnificent pro- duction by

"Untwifting all the chains that tie
"The hidden foul of harmony."

*E   P A R T

P A R T II.

O V E R T U R E   I N   S A U L.

Compofed in 1740.

THE firft movement of this admirable compofition, fo different from the common ftyle of Overture, which Lulli
had eftablifhed, and to which all the compofers in Europe, for
more than fifty years, implicitly conformed, is extremely pleafing;
and when it was firft heard, muft have furprifed, by the grace
and novelty of its conduct and paffages.

Though the reft of this Overture was fuperfeded, in favour of
the *Dead March*, yet it is but juftice to the author to fay, that
the fecond movement, with folo parts for the principal hautbois
and violin, is fo *chantant*, as perpetually to remind the hearer of
a vocal duet, richly accompanied. The fugue, indeed, with folo
parts for the organ, was, perhaps, very judicioufly omitted; as
the paffages have been long in fuch favour with the imitators of
HANDEL, as to be rendered trite and vulgar. The *Minuet* will,
however, always preferve its grace and dignity; being one of the
few final movements of an Overture, which neither age, nor fafhion, can deform.

THE DEAD MARCH IN SAUL.

This moft happy and affecting movement, which has retained
its favour near half a century, and which is fo fimple, folemn,
and forrowful, that it can never be heard, even upon a fingle inftrument,

ftrument, without exciting melancholy fenfations, received here all the dignity and grandeur which it could poffibly derive from the various tones of the moft powerful, as well as beft difciplined, band, that was ever affembled.

PART OF THE ANTHEM WHICH WAS PERFORMED IN WESTMINSTER ABBEY AT THE FUNERAL OF HER SA-CERD MAJESTY QUEEN CAROLINE, 1737.

" *When the ear heard her, then it bleffed her ; and when the eye faw her, it gave witnefs of her.*" Job xxix. 11.

This elegant, mild, and forrowing ftrain, after all the riot-ous clangor of jubilation in the *Te Deum,* and powerful per-cuffion of drums, and tuneful blafts of trumpets and facbuts, in the Dead March, was foothing and comforting to the ear. Contraft is the great fource of our mufical pleafure ; for however delighted we may be with *quick, flow, loud,* or *foft,* for a certain time, variety is fo neceffary to ftimulate attention, that the per-formance which is in want of the one, is never fure of the other. This charming movement is ftill fo new, that it would do honour to the tafte, as well as knowledge in harmony, of any compofer now living. HANDEL had a verfatile genius ; and, if he had con-tinued to write for the Opera, inftead of the Church, there was no elegance or refinement which Haffe, Vinci, Pergolefi, and their fucceffors, ever attained, that was out of his reach.

" *She delivered the poor that cried, the fatherlefs, and him that* " *had none to help him.*—Job xxix. 12. *Kindnefs, meeknefs, and* " *comfort were in her tongue* ; Ecclef. xxxvi. 23. *If there was* " *any virtue, aud if there was any praife, fhe thought on thofe* " *things.*" Phil. iv. 8.

F

The

The trebles finging alone, and only accompanied in unifon, by treble inftruments, at the words—" *kindnefs, meeknefs, and* " *comfort were in her tongue,*" had an admirable effect, in point of contraft, with the full harmony of the reft of this charming Chorus. Indeed, this *Nænia* contains all the requifites of good Mufic, in plain counterpoint : as good harmony, melody, rhythm, accent, and expreffion *(a)*. The beauties of this ftrain are of every age and country ; no change of fafhion can efface them, or prevent their being felt by perfons of fenfibility.

" *Their bodies are buried in peace ;*" Ecclef. xliv. 14.

This admirable fragment of folemn and forrowful harmony, in the Church ftyle, almoft wholly without inftruments, is an excellent introduction to the lefs plaintive ftrain which follows :

" *But their name liveth evermore ;*" Ibid.

which is one of the moft fingular and agreeable Chorufes I know, and was performed with an accuracy, power, and fpirit, which neither that, nor, perhaps, any Mufic of the kind ever received before *(b)*. Each of the three movements from the *Funeral Anthem,* feemed to excite fuch lively fenfations of grief, as reminded all

---

(a) There are likewife fome natural and pleafing imitations in the latter part of the movement, which, however, neither deftroy the accent, nor render the words unintelligible, the crimes ufually laid to the charge of *Canons, Fugues,* and *Imitations.* But HANDEL, who felt, and fo well expreffed the *general fentiments* of the words he fet to Mufic in our language, was never certain of their *pronunciation :* the word *delivered,* which is generally, by elifion, made a *trifyllable,* had never, I believe, been contracted to a *diffyllable,* before ; but in this Chorus, though the word is very often re-

peated, never more than *two notes* were allowed to it.

(b) In this, and the preceding movement, HANDEL has made a happy ufe of a modulation which was very frequent in the fixteenth century : the giving a common chord to the flat feventh of a major key, juft before a clofe. The laws of *liaifon,* or relation, which have been fince eftabl'fhed, have ban'fhed this modulation from fecular Mufic ; but in that of the Church, when fparingly ufed, it is not only allowable, but productive of fine effects.

present

prefent of the ravages which death had made among their parti-cular families and friends, and moved many even to tears.

GLORIA PATRI. From the Jubilate, 1713.

" Glory be to the Father," &c.

This Chorus, from the *Jubilate*, which HANDEL fet at the fame time as the grand *Te Deum*, for the peace at Utrecht, and the only *Jubilate* he ever compofed, being in his grandeft and moft magnificent ftyle, received every poffible advantage in the per-formance, from a correct and powerful band, and the moft mute and eager attention in the audience.

P A R T   III.

ANTHEM.   Compofed about the Year 1719.

AIR AND CHORUS.

" *O fing unto the Lord a new fong*; *O fing unto the Lord all*
the whole earth."   Pf. xcvi. 1.

MADAME Mara's voice and manner of finging in this plain
and folemn air, fo admirably accompanied on the hautbois by Fifher, had a fudden effect on myfelf, which I never before experienced, even from her performance of more pathetic
Mufic.   I have long admired her voice, and abilities in various
ftyles of finging; but never imagined tendernefs the peculiar cha-
racteriftic of her performance : however, here, though fhe had
but a few fimples notes to deliver, they made me fhiver, and I
found it extremely difficult to avoid burfting into tears on hearing
them.   Indeed, fhe had not only the power of conveying to the
remoteft corner of this immenfe building, the fofteft and moft
artificial inflexions of her fweet and brilliant voice, but articulated every fyllable of the words with fuch neatnefs, precifion,
and purity, that it was rendered as audible, and intelligible, as it
could poffibly have been, in a fmall theatre, by meer declamation.

CHORUS.

" *Declare his honour unto the Heathen, and his wonders unto all*
" *people—For the Lord is great, and cannot worthily be praifed.*"
Pf. xcvi. 3, 4.

This

This Chorus is in a truly grand ſtyle, and produced great effects though there are only three vocal parts. The ſubject is reverſed, at the latter end, in a moſt ingenious manner.

"*He is more to be feared than all gods.*" Pſ. xcvi. 3, 4.

Here the modulation is ſublime, and truly eccleſiaſtic. The pauſe on E ♭ with a perfect chord, the inſtant before a cloſe in F, carries us again to the ſixteenth century *(a)*.

"*The waves of the ſea rage horribly ; but yet the Lord who dwells on high is mightier.*" Pſ. xciii. 5.

HANDEL, in the accompaniments of this boiſterous air, has tried, not unſuccesfully, to expreſs the turbulence of a tempeſ-tuous ſea ; the ſtyle of this kind of Muſic is not meant to be amiable ; but it contraſts well with other movements, and this has a ſpirit, and even roughneſs, peculiar to our author.

D U E T.

"*O worſhip the Lord in the beauty of holineſs.*" Pſ. xcvi. 9.

The ſolemnity of this movement may, perhaps, ſeem as much too languid to the admirers of the preceding air, as that may be too turbulent for the nerves of thoſe who are partial to this. The truth is, that both verge a little on the extreme ; but a compoſer, of ſuch extenſive powers of invention as HANDEL, dares every thing, for the ſake of variety : and this Duet is much in the ad-mired ſtyle of Steffani.

(a) Arkadelt, the moſt celebrated ma-drigaliſt of that period, in a favourite ma-drigal beginning : *Il bianco e dolce cigno can-tando muore*, has the ſame modulation im-mediately preceding a cloſe.

CHORUS.

C H O R U S.

" *Let all the whole earth ſtand in awe of him.* Ibid.   *Let the*
" *heavens rejoice, and let the earth be glad; let the ſea make a*
" *noiſe and all that therein is.*"   Ibid. 11.

In the laſt movement of this Chorus, when all the inſtruments
are buſied, ſuch a commotion is raiſed, as conſtitutes one of
HANDEL's moſt formidable hurricanes.

" Bellowing *notes* burſt with a ſtormy ſound."   ADDISON.

CHORUS IN ISRAEL IN EGYPT.
Compoſed in 1738.

" *The Lord ſhall reign for ever and ever.*"   Exod. xv. 18.

This moſt admirable compoſition which is written *a due cori*,
begins by the tenors and counter-tenors, in uniſon, accompanied
only by a ground baſe.

R E C I T A T I V E.

" *For the horſe of Pharaoh with his chariots,*" &c. Exod. xv.

Mr. Norris pronounced this and the following Recitative with
the true energy of an Engliſhman, who perfectly comprehended
and articulated the words.

C H O R U S.

" *The Lord ſhall reign for ever and ever.*"

The return to this ſhort ſtrain of Chorus, after each fragment
of Recitative, has a fine effect.

R E C I T A T I V E.

" *And Miriam the propheteſs, the ſiſter of Aaron, took a timbrel*
" *in her hand: and all the women went out after her with timbrels*
" *and with dances.*"   Exod. xv. 19.

CHORUS.

CHORUS.

" *Sing ye to the Lord, for he hath triumphed gloriously (a).* The
" *Lord shall reign for ever and ever. The horse and his rider he*
" *hath thrown into the sea."* Exod. xv. 21.

The effects of this composition are at once pleasing, grand, and sublime! The aggregate of voices and instruments had here its full effect. And such is the excellence of this production, that if HANDEL had composed no other piece, this alone would have rendered his name immortal, among true lovers and judges of harmony *(b)*.

(a) HANDEL's uncertainty in whatever concerned the accent and pronunciation of our language appears very remarkably in his manner of setting this last Chorus; where he accents the words, " *For he hath* " *triumphed gloriously,"* thus : " *Fŏr hĕ hăth triŭmphĕd glŏriŏuſly."* But in the year 1738, when he composed the Oratorio of *Iſrael in Egypt,* our language was not very familiar to him; and he had then but little experience in ſetting it to Muſic.

(b) The art with which HANDEL, in the midſt of all the fire of imagination and ebullition of genius, introduces a ſober, *chanting* kind of *counter-ſubject,* while the other is carried on with uninterrupted ſpirit, is marvellous! (See printed Score, p. 265.) after giving this new ſubject alternately to different ſingle parts, and ſometimes to two parts in thirds, without diminiſhing the activity of the reſt, which are continuing the general Chorus, he for a few bars (p. 277) makes this the principal vocal ſubject; and after being led off by the baſe, a regular reply is made by the other parts, in the fifth and octave. However, the inſtruments never let the firſt ſubject be forgotten, but contrive to play fragments of it, in accompanying the voices, during five bars that they are employed, ſolely, by the ſecond ſubject. After

which the firſt theme is reſumed, and continued to the end, by all the Nineteen parts of this multifarious ſcore. I ſhould not have been ſo minute in my analyſis of this Chorus, if it were not to point out a diſcovery which I made in peruſing the ſcore, and to which the performance, in the midſt of the pleaſure I received from it, had not led me. The diſcovery 1 mean is, that the intervals in this counter-ſubject are exactly the ſame as in the celebrated canon, *Non Nobis Domine.*

I will ſing   un-to the Lord.
Whether the ſubject occurred to HANDEL accidentally, or was taken with deſign, I know not; but in either caſe, the notes are happily ſelected, and ingeniouſly uſed. As to the *original inventor,* or *right owner* of that ſeries of notes upon which the canon, which tradition has given to Bird, was conſtructed, they had been the ſubject of fugue to Zarlino, and to old Adrian Villaert, his maſter, long before Bird was born; and, indeed, conſtitute one of the different ſpecies of *tetrachord,* uſed by the Greeks, in the higheſt antiquity.

Upon

Upon the whole, the fuccefs of this day's performance may, with the utmoft truth, be pronounced entire; as its effects furpaffed the moft fanguine expectations of the greateft enthufiafts for the honour of HANDEL, the glory of the profeffion, and profperity of this grand enterprife. And, indeed, he muft have been not only a faftidious, but a very ignorant and infenfible hearer, who did not receive new and exquifite pleafure from the compofition and execution of the pieces which were this day performed.

But, in juftice to the audience, it may be faid, that though the frequency of hearing good Mufic in this capital, of late years, has fo far blunted the edge of curiofity and appetite, that the beft Operas and Concerts are accompanied with a buz and murmur of converfation, equal to that of a tumultuous croud, or the din of high 'Change; yet now, fuch a ftillnefs reigned, as, perhaps, never happened before in fo large an affembly. The midnight hour was never founded in more perfect tranquillity, than every note of thefe compofitions. I have long been watching the operations of good Mufic on the fenfibility of mankind; but never remember, in any part of Europe, where I attended Mufical exhibitions, in the Church, Theatre, or Chamber, to have obferved fo much curiofity excited, attention beftowed, or fatisfaction glow in the countenances of thofe prefent, as on this occafion. The effects, indeed, upon many were fuch as modern times have never before experienced. The *Choral power* of harmonical combinations affected fome to tears, and fainting; while others were melted and enrapt, by the exquifite fweetnefs of *fingle founds*. I had little leifure to contemplate the countenances of thofe around me; but, when I happened to turn my eyes from the performers, I faw nothing but tears of extacy, and looks of wonder and delight.

Indeed,

Nothing, however, difcovered the admirable difcipline of the band, and unwearied and determined attention of the audience, fo much as the *paufes*, which are fo frequent in HANDEL's Mufic : for thefe were fo unanimoufly calculated, and meafured, that no pla-toon, or fingle cannon, was ever fired with more exact precifion or unity of effect, than that with which the whole phalanx of this multitudinous band refumed its work, after all the fudden, and ufually, unlimited ceffations of found, commonly called *paufes*, which, in general, catch loquacity in the fact; but now, at all thefe unexpected moments, the filence was found as awful and entire, as if none but the tombs of departed mortals had been prefent.

G   COM-

FROM HARMONY, FROM HEAVENLY HARMONY THIS UNIVERSAL FRAME BEGAN

HANDEL

J. R. Cipriani R. A. Invent.

F. Bartolozzi R. A. Engraver to his Majesty Sc.

HANDEL composing sacred Music; the Genius of Harmony crowning him, & a Seraph wafting his name to heaven.

COMMEMORATION

O F

HANDEL.

SECOND PERFORMANCE,

PANTHEON.

THURSDAY EVENING, May 27, 1784.

G 2

LIST of the Pieces selected for the Second Performance.

PART I.

SECOND HAUTBOIS CONCERTO.
Sorge infausta, AIR in ORLANDO.
Ye Sons of Israel—CHORUS in JOSHUA.
Rende il sereno—AIR in SOSARMES.
Caro vieni—in RICHARD THE FIRST.
He smote all the first-born. CHORUS, from ISRAEL IN EGYPT.
Va tacito e nascosto. AIR in JULIUS CÆSAR.
SIXTH GRAND CONCERTO.
M'allontano sdegnose pupille. AIR in ATALANTA.
He gave them hail-stones for rain. CHORUS—ISRAEL IN
EGYPT.

PART II.

FIFTH GRAND CONCERTO.
Dite che fà—AIR in PTOLEMY.
Vi fida lo sposo—in ÆTIUS.
Fallen is the foe, CHORUS, in JUDAS MACCHABÆUS.

OVERTURE OF ARIADNE.
Alma del gran Pompeo. Accompanied Recitative in JULIUS
CÆSAR.

Followed by
Affanni del pensier— AIR in OTHO.
Nasco al bosco — —- in ÆTIUS.
Io t'abbraccio —DUET in RODELINDA.

ELEVENTH GRAND CONCERTO.
Ah! mio cor!—AIR in ALCINA.
ANTHEM. *My heart is inditing of a good matter.*

THE company, to-night, aſſembled very early, for fear of not gaining admiſſion, and the croud was exceſſive. Though the doors were not to be opened till Six o'clock, yet great numbers of well-dreſſed people preſented themſelves at the entrance from Oxford-ſtreet, before that time; and, by Seven, though the performance was not to begin till Eight, the whole building was ſo full, that not another place could be obtained, on any terms. The extreme heat of the weather, augmented by the animal heat of more than Sixteen hundred people, cloſely wedged together, muſt have conſiderably diminiſhed the delight which the lovers of Muſic expected to receive from this night's exhibition: when the body ſuffers, the mind is very difficult to be pleaſed.

The unexpected ſucceſs, and wonderful effects, of the firſt performance in the Abbey, had made impreſſions, and raiſed expectations in the public, which, on the reduced ſcale that the inferior ſize of the building required, were not likely to be ſatisfied. Great concerts had often been heard in the Pantheon, and great crouds of the firſt people in the kingdom, ſeen there before. And though the band was at leaſt four times more numerous than ordinary, at this place, yet it was ſo inferior, in number and effect, to that at the Abbey, that expectation ſeemed generally diſappointed. The character and variety of the pieces, however, did as much honour to HANDEL, and to the ſelector of them, as their execution did to the performers.

This

This moſt elegant building ſo far ſurpaſſes, in beauty, any other place appropriated to public amuſements, throughout Europe, that it is infinitely more the wonder of foreigners, than natives ; and yet theſe, however often they may have ſeen it, ſtill regard it with freſh admiration ; and though it was natural to think it impoſſible that any thing could be added to the ſplendor of this ſtructure, the original architect, Mr. James Wyatt, ſo happily exerciſed his creative genius in the preparations for the reception of their Majeſties and the company, that we ſhall preſent our readers with the following deſcription of them.

The eaſt and weſt galleries, and the paſſages behind the colonade, as well as the gallery over the orcheſtra, were filled up with benches, for company. In this gallery there was a new organ-caſe, decorated with a tranſparent portrait of HANDEL, from an original painting, preſented to the Concert of Ancient Muſic by Mr. Redmond Simpſon, with boys in *chiaro oſcuro*, holding a wreath of laurel. The Orcheſtra was conſiderably enlarged. Over the entrance into the Pantheon, oppoſite the Orcheſtra, was erected a gallery, ſupported by ſix Ionic columns, like thoſe of the original building. In the center of this gallery was placed their Majeſty's box, lined with crimſon ſattin, and ornamented with looking-glaſs. It was hung with curtains of crimſon damaſk, fringed with gold. The cieling was elegantly painted in Mr. Wyatt's uſual ſtyle of ornamental painting. The box was covered with a dome, in which were placed the royal ſupporters, in gold. Behind their Majeſty's box, were ſeats for their attendants ; and, on one ſide, for the Directors and their friends ; and, on the other, for the maids of honour. The front of the royal box was decorated with crimſon curtains and valances, fringed and laced with gold. The great dome of the Pantheon was illuminated with additional lamps,

innu-

innumerable ; and, as this was the firſt performance here, that was honoured by the preſence of their Majeſties, not only the decorations, but the ſplendor of the company, exceeded whatever this beautiful building could boaſt before.

The band of to-night, conſiſting of two hundred of the moſt ſelect performers who had been employed in the Abbey, with the addition of ſignor Paccherotti, the firſt ſinger at the Opera, among the vocal, was led by Mr. Cramer, with his accuſtomed attention and fire. And as the performances in Weſtminſter-Abbey manifeſted, in a wonderful manner, HANDEL's great powers, as an *Eccleſiaſtical* Compoſer, this evening's exhibition was judiciouſly calculated to diſplay his abilities in *Secular*, and *Dramatic*, Muſic.

PART

PART I.

SECOND HAUTBOIS CONCERTO.

THIS Compofition, played as an Overture to the whole performance, had an admirable effect. The opening is remarkably grand, and accented; and the Largo, with Solo parts for two Violoncellos, and a cantabile part for the Hautbois, quietly accompanied, is very rich in harmony and contrivance; but the double fugue, which firft appeared among HANDEL's Organ fugues, is upon two of the moft pleafing fubjects, and treated, perhaps, in the moft clear and mafterly manner, of any inftrumental fugue that has ever been compofed. The Minuet and Gavot have confiderable merit, of a lighter kind, and long delighted the frequenters of our theatres and public places *(a)*.

The fet of pieces, of which this is one, though called *Hautbois Concertos*, has very few folo parts for that inftrument; moft of the divifions, and difficult paffages, being affigned to the principal Violin. Indeed thefe compofitions, which are more in the ftyle of Haydn's Symphonies, than modern Hautbois Concertos, with long folo parts for the difplay of abilities on that particular inftrument, are admirably calculated for a large and powerful band, in which there are performers on various inftruments, who merit diftinction.

(a) The Hautbois part of this bold and mafterly Concerto was played by Mr. Kellner, of his Majefty's military band; a fcholar of Mr. Fifcher, who, by his tone and execution, manifefted himfelf to be a worthy difciple of fo great a mafter.

AIR

AIR IN ORLANDO.

Compofed 1732.

SIGNOR TASCA.

Sorge infaufta una procella
  Che ofcurar fa il cielo e il mare,
  Splende faufta poi la ftella,
  Che ogni cor ne fà goder.

Può talor il forte errare
  Ma riforto dall' errore,
  Quel, che pria gli diè dolore
  Caufa immenfo il fuo piacer.

Though furious ftorms awhile may rage,
And darknefs ev'ry hope deny,
The Sun, at length, fhall fear affuage,
And calm at once the heart and fky.

So men, endow'd with virtue rare,
The lures of vice fometimes decoy;
Yet, freed from each infidious fnare,
Converfion brings unbounded joy.

This is an Air abounding in that fpecies of ingenious and maf-terly contrivance, which generally delights the eye and judg-ment of deep Muficians, much more than the public ear. An Opera, however, without fuch fpecimens of mufical fcience, is never had in much reverence by profeffors. But, fo changed is the ftyle of Dramatic Mufic, fince HANDEL's was produced, that almoft all his fongs feem *fcientific*.

H   CHORUS

CHORUS IN JOSHUA,

First performed 1747.

" *Ye sons of Israel, every tribe attend,*
" *Let grateful Songs and Hymns to Heaven ascend;*
" *In Gilgal, and on Jordan's banks proclaim*
" *One First, one Great, one Lord Jehovah's name."*

This Chorus, unexpectedly bursting out of the second movement of the Overture, is of a very beautiful and singular kind. The first part, to the words, " *Let grateful Songs and Hymns to Hea-*
" *ven ascend,"* is lively and chearful, without vulgarity, and the points of imitation new and pleasing; but in the last part, at the words, " *In Gilgal, and on Jordan's banks proclaim, one First,*
" *one Great, one Lord Jehovah's name,"* the composition is truly grand, and sublime; uniting propriety of expression with as much learning and ingenuity of fugue, modulation, accompaniment, and texture of parts, as the art of Music can boast.

AIR IN SOSARMES.

Composed 1732.

Mr. HARRISON.

Rendi il sereno al ciglio
  Madre, non pianger più,
  Temer d'alcun periglio
  Oggi mai come puoi tù.

May heav'n in pity smooth that brow,
And dry a tender parent's tear;
Nor e'er again her heart allow
To swell with sorrow so severe.

This

This is a ſhort, but pathetic, and ſoothing ſtrain, in a ſlow Siciliana movement, which HANDEL ſeldom fails to make intereſting. I have been told that Strada, for whom this air was originally compoſed, captivated the audience extremely, by her performance of it. Few are now alive who can remember by what peculiar powers of voice or expreſſion ſhe delighted the public in this ſong, fifty-two years ago; though many are the hands that bore teſtimony to the accuracy, purity, and propriety, with which it was ſung by Mr. Harriſon, on the preſent occaſion.

AIR IN RICHARD THE FIRST.

Compoſed 1727.

Miſs CANTELO.

Caro vieni, vieni a me,
Fido vieni; puoi tu caro
Adolcire il duolo amaro
Di chi pena ſol per te.

Penſa, penſa alla mia fè,
Penſa ancor al mio martir,
Ed a tanti miei ſoſpir
Sarai ſolo la mercè.

Ah! come, and kindly eaſe my heart
Of all its pains, of all its fears;
Ah! faithful come, and joy impart,
Nor longer leave me thus in tears.

Think of my conſtancy and love,
Think of my unremitting woes;
Ah! come in ſmiles, and inſtant prove
How well, for thee, I loſt repoſe.

This

This is an innocent, fimple kind of Air, which requires no great abilities to perform, or fcience to hear. A pleafing well-toned voice, free from the Englifh brogue and vulgarity, is all that is neceffary to the finger; and a difpofition to be pleafed with mufical tones, to the hearer. Mifs Cantelo certainly brought the one to the Pantheon, and found the other there. Nothing can prove more clearly the difference of ftyle in finging this fpecies of Air, fifty years ago, than the fhake which Cuzzoni made on the firft note, and almoft always on the word *caro*, wherever it occurred. A good fhake, well applied, is certainly one of the firft embellifhments of good finging; but when injudicioufly ufed, it is pert and unmeaning. Shakes are now fparingly ufed by the few who are able to make them, except at a clofe, and in old-fafhioned French finging.

CHORUS, FROM ISRAEL IN EGYPT.

Compofed 1738.

" *He fmote all the firft-born of Egypt, the chief of all their*
" *ftrength*, Pf. lxxvii. 52. *But as for his people, he led them forth*
" *like fheep*, Ibid. 53. *He brought them out with filver and gold,*
" *there was not one feeble perfon in all their tribes.*" Pf. cv. 36.

Unimpaffioned narrative fupplies a compofer with few opportunities of mufical expreffion, or with that fpecies of imitation, where the *found* can, with propriety, be made *an echo* to the fenfe. But HANDEL, in the firft movement of this admirable Chorus on two pleafing and uncommon fubjects, in the accompaniments, which only mark the accented parts of each bar, has excited an idea of *fmiting*, and of *blows*. And in the courfe of this clofe and

regular

regular double fugue, when he gives the inftruments more to do, he produces the fame effects by fhort elementary founds affigned to the voices, in plain counterpoint. The fecond movement; " *He* " *led them forth like fheep,*" is of a paftoral caft, with a mixture of fugue, and a termination, in clofe, compact, and well arranged full harmony, of fyllabic counterpoint, or note againft note.

AIR IN JULIUS CÆSAR.

Compofed in 1723.

Signor PACCHIEROTTI.

Va tacito e nafcofto
  Quand' avido è di preda
  L' aftuto cacciator.

Così chi è al mal difpofto,
  Non brama, ch' alcun veda
  L'Inganno del fuo cor.

The wiley fportfman in purfuit of game,
Unfeen, and filent, takes his aim ;
So he whom malice prompts to bafe defigns,
With equal art, his plans combines.

Whoever is able to read a *fcore,* and knows the difficulty of writing in five real parts, muft admire the refources which HANDEL has manifefted in this. The French-horn part, which is almoft a perpetual echo to the voice, has never been equalled in any Air, fo accompanied, that I remember. Few great fingers are partial to fongs in which the melody and importance are fo equally divided ; but this Air was chofen to do honour to the abilities of HANDEL, on a day when they were to fhine in full fplendor.

And

And ſignor Pacchierotti, by his judicious choice and excellent performance, at once contributed to the blaze of this great com-poſer's reputation, and his own.

SIXTH GRAND CONCERTO.

The firſt movement is ſolemn and ſorrowful; and the fugue, remarkably curious in ſubjeƈt; which is ſo unobvious and diffi-cult to work, that no compoſer of ordinary abilities, in this learned ſpecies of writing, would have ventured to meddle with it, if ſuch an unnatural ſeries of ſounds had occurred to him. The muſette, or, rather chaconne, in this Concerto, was always in fa-vour with the compoſer himſelf, as well as the public; for I well remember, that HANDEL frequently introduced it between the parts of his Oratorios, both before and after publication. In-deed, no inſtrumental compoſition which I had ever heard during the long favour of this, ſeemed to me more grateful and pleaſing, particularly, in ſubjeƈt : the ſolo parts and diviſions were not very new, at the time they occurred to HANDEL in this movement; but, probably, they render the return to the firſt theme the more welcome. To the reſt of the Concerto, which was omitted in this performance, little praiſe is due, and, indeed, this ſeemed to be HANDEL's own opinion; as the two laſt movements were frequently omitted in performance, under his own direƈtion.

A I R

AIR IN ATALANTA.

Compofed 1736.

MADAME MARA.

M'allontano fdegnofe pupille
Per vedervi più liete, e ferene,
E perch' abbian le voftre faville
Nudrimento minore di pene.

Awhile I retire from your fcorn and difdain,
Nor with fpleen or refentment upbraid;
In hopes that by love, both my patience and pain
Will, with int'reft, in future be paid.

This Air, which was originally fet for the celebrated Conti, *detto Gizziello,* from Gizzi, a famous finger, and, afterwards, finging-mafter, of whom he learned his art, though it requires in the finger no uncommon extent of voice, pathos, or execution, yet, by the grace, elegant fimplicity, and fweetnefs, as well as power of voice, with which Madame Mara fung this pleafing fong, fhe fortified the great reputation which fhe brought into this country, and which fhe had realized, and fo much increafed, by her performance in Weftminfter-Abbey. This Air, in which the bafe and other accompaniments are as quiet and fimple as thofe of Haffe and Vinci, of the fame period; fhews, that when HANDEL chofe to make the finger more important than the Orcheftra, the tafk was not difficult.

CHORUS

CHORUS IN ISRAEL IN EGYPT.

Compofed 1738.

" *He gave them hailftones for rain* ; Pf. cv. 32. *Fire mingled*
" *with the hail, ran along upon the ground.*" Exod. ix. 23, 24.

This fpirited and mafterly movement, which was clamoroufly
called for, a fecond time, is written *a due Cori*. It is one of the
few Chorufes, compofed by HANDEL, in which there is no
fugue, or point of imitation, except in the echos of the two choirs;
but, *en revanche*, the inftrumental parts are fo active, and full,
without occafioning the leaft confufion, that, if the eight voice
parts were filent, the accompaniments might be played with good
effect, as a movement in a Concerto : a circumftance difficult to
point out, in the works of any other compofer, than HANDEL.

PART

PART II.

FIFTH GRAND CONCERTO.

THE opening of this piece always impreffed me with the idea of its being the moft fpirited and charaçteriftic of all the movements that were written by HANDEL, or any other com-pofer, on Lulli's model of Opera Overture; which feems to require a convulfive, determined, and military caft. The two following movements, of which only the firft was played, con-tain little more than the light and common-place paffages of the times. The *Largo*, however, is an excellent piece of harmony and modulation, in Corelli's natural and fober ftyle; and, in the next movement, we have a very early fpecimen of the fymphonic ftyle of Italy, in which rapid iterations of the fame note are de-figned to contraft with fomething better, if not mere noife and *rempliffage*, totally devoid of meaning, of which there are but too frequent inftances. The fubjeçt of HANDEL's movement is modern, marked, and pleafing; and the bafe accompaniment of his iterations, bold and interefting. The finale, or minuet of this Concerto, has been fo much admired by Englifh compofers of HANDEL's fchool, as to have been frequently thought worthy of imitation.

I   AIR

AIR IN PTOLEMY.

Compofed 1728.

Mifs ABRAMS.

Dite che fà
   Dove è l'idol mio,
   Selvaggie deità
   Dite dov' è
   Il mio teforo ?
A me voi lo rendete
   O pur fè lo vedete
   Ditegli per pietà
   Che per lui moro.
O rendetelo al mio cor ;
   Dite che tutto amor,
   Sofpiro anch' io.

Where is my Love ? and how employ'd ?
Ye Fauns and Dryads fay ;
If to your rural haunts decoy'd,
Aloud repeat my lay.

In pity tell him ev'ry pain,
Each groan and rifing figh ;
That far from him I life difdain,
And only wifh to die.

Ye ruftic gods, oh tell him this,
Or bring him here to crown my blifs.
Where is my Love ? &c.

This air, which is pleafing, and modern in melody, for one that has fifty-fix years on its head, is called the *Echo Song*, in the printed copy ; and faid to have been fung by Signora Cuzzoni, and Signor Senefino. So few paffages, however, are repeated,

and

and thofe chiefly in the fecond part, that it had a very good effect, as a folo fong, from the tafte and expreffion with which it was fung by Mifs Abrams.

AIR IN EZIO, or ÆTIUS.

Compofed 1732.

Signor BARTOLINI.

Vi fida lo fpofo
Vi fida il regnante,
Dubbiofo,
Ed amante
La vita,
E l'amor.
Tu, amico, prepara
Soccorfo, ed aita:
Tu ferbami, O cara,
Gli affetti del cor.

To thee I confide
My empire and bride;
And, in doubt while I rove,
My life, and my love :—
Do thou, my dear friend,
Affiftance prepare—
While on thee I depend
Thy affection to fhare.

This Air, which is in a ftyle peculiar to HANDEL, and the period in which he flourifhed, has, perhaps, been robbed a little of its beauty and grace, by time; it, however, filled up its niche in the Pantheon, with the affiftance of Signor Bartolini, very agreeably. For my own part, who wifh that whatever is good in its

I 2   kind

kind may live, and have a fhare of attention and favour, I confefs, that a compofition is the more curious, and welcome to my ears, in proportion as it *differs* from the Mufic in common ufe.

CHORUS IN JUDAS MACCHABÆUS,

Compofed 1746.

Fall'n is the foe,
So fall thy foes, O Lord,
Where warlike Judas wields his righteous fword.

This fpirited, original, and excellent Chorus, which can never pafs without honourable notice in any performance, received great force and energy from the manner in which it was executed to-night.

OVERTURE IN ARIADNE.

Compofed 1734.

The great favour which this Overture fo long enjoyed, particularly the *Minuet*, was here revived, and a new leafe of longevity granted to it by HANDEL's *executors.* The number of French horns employed on this occafion very much enriched the harmony, and gave to the effect of this Air, unufual fplendor and magnificence.

ACCOMPANIED RECITATIVE IN JULIUS CÆSAR.

Compofed 1723.

Signor PACCHIEROTTI.

Alma del gran Pompeo,
Che al cener fuo d'intorno

Invifibil

Invisibil t'aggiri,
Fur ombra i tuoi trofei,
Ombra la tua grandezza, e un ombra sei!
Così termina al fine il fasto umano!
Jeri chi vivo occupò un mondo in guerra,
Oggi, risolto in polve, un urna serra!
Tal di ciascuno, ahi lasso!
Il principio è di terra
E il fine un sasso!
Misera vita! O quanto è fral tuo stato!
Ti forma un soffio, e ti distrugge un fiato.

Thefe are thy afhes, Pompey, this the mound,
Thy foul, invifible, is hovering round!
Thy fplendid trophies, and thy honours fade,
Thy grandeur, like thyfelf, is now a fhade.
Thus fare the hopes in which we moſt confide,
And thus the efforts end of human pride!
What yeſterday could hold the world in chains,
To-day, transform'd to duſt, an urn contains.
Such is the fate of all, from cot to throne,
Our origin is earth, our end a ſtone!
Ah wretched life! how frail and fhort thy joys!
A breath creates thee, and a breath deſtroys.

This admirable foliloquy of Cæfar over the afhes of Pompey, I have been frequently told by perfons equally well fkilled in Mufic and the Italian tongue, had an effect, when recited on the ſtage by Senefino, which no Recitative, or even Air, had before, in this country. But though delivered by Signor Pacchierotti, with the true energy and expreffion of heroic Recitative, for which he is fo much celebrated in Italy by the beſt judges of the poetry and mufical declamation of that country, had not the attention

tention or fuccefs it deferved here, detached from its place in the
Opera, and printed without a tranflation.   Indeed, the audience,
fatigued with the ftruggles for admiffion, the preffure of the croud
in their feats, and relaxed by the accumulated heat of the weather and company, were neither fo attentive to the performers,
nor willing to be pleafed by their exertions, as in Weftminfter-
Abbey.

RECITATIVE, which Englifhmen, unacquainted with the
Italian language, always wifh as fhort as poffible, is thought of
fuch importance, in Italy, that it feems to include the carriage and
geftures, as well as elocution of an Opera finger : for when it is
faid of one, *recita bene*, it is underftood that *he*, or *fhe*, not only
fpeaks Recitative well, but is a good *actor*, or *actrefs*.

Tartini *(a)* gives an account of a piece of Recitative that was performed in an Opera at Ancona, in 1714, which had a very extraordinary effect on the profeffors employed in it, as well as the audience ;
for though it had no other accompaniment than a bafe, and confifted of only one line, it occafioned fuch agitation in all who
heard it, that they trembled, turned pale, and regarded each other
with fear and aftonifhment.   And thefe extraordinary effects did not
arife from complaints, forrow, or tragic pathos of any uncommon
kind ; but from indignation, and an undefinable fpecies of rigid feverity and penetrating harfhnefs in the fentiments of the words, the
power of which was greatly augmented and enforced, both by the
compofer and performer.   " During thirteen reprefentations of
" this Drama," continues the intelligent and excellent Mufician
who has recorded thefe powers of Recitative, " the effect was
" ftill the fame ; and, after the firft night, this terrible fcene was
" conftantly expected with the moft profound filence."

(a) Trattato di Mufica, cap. v. p. 135.

An

An attention little inferior to this, according to tradition, was bestowed upon the scene in Julius Cæsar, when performed in England. The translation may, perhaps, convey some faint idea of the original words; nothing, however, but the Music itself, and the recitation of such a performer as Senesino, or Pacchierotti, can do justice to HANDEL's merit in setting them. Indeed, it is the finest piece of accompanied Recitative, without intervening symphonies, with which I am acquainted. The modulation is learned, and so uncommon, that there is hardly a chord which the ear expects; and yet the words are well expressed, and the phrases pathetic and pleasing.

This Recitative was followed by one of HANDEL's most cele-brated pathetic Airs:

A I R I N O T H O,
Composed 1722.
Signor PACCHIEROTTI.

Affanni del penfier,
Un fol momento,
Datemi pace almen
E poi tornate.
Ah! che nel mefto fen
Io gia vi fento
Che oftinati la pace,
A me turbate.

Afflicting thoughts, a fhort reprieve
In pity grant,
And then return;
But ah! for ever, I perceive,
My heart will pant
My bofom burn.

This

This exquifite Air was compofed for Cuzzoni. Both the fong, and her performance of it, were greatly admired by the beft judges of the times ; and it is not, perhaps, eafy to find an Air of greater merit in any one of HANDEL's Italian operas.   The melody is purely Sicilian ; and though the inftrumental parts are moving in ftrict fugue, almoft throughout, it is as free and unembarraffed, as if it was accompanied in fimple counterpoint.   It is fo high as not to be in the pleafanteft part of Signor Pacchierotti's voice : and, though he fung it with great feeling and expreffion, it was not tafted by the audience in the manner it deferved.

A I R   I N   E Z I O.

Compofed 1732.

Signor T A S C A.

Nafce al bofco in rozza cuna
*   Un felice paftorello,*
*   E con l'aure di fortuna,*
*   Giunge i regni a dominar.*
Preffo al trono in regie fafce
*   Sventurato un altro nafce,*
*   E fra l'ire della forte,*
*   Va gli armenti a pafcolar.*

Sometimes a happy ruftic fwain,
In cottage born, of humble ftem,
Acquires with little toil and pain,
Through Fortune's fmiles, a diadem.
While he that's blafted by her frown
To dire mifchance is fure decreed ;
And, though entitled to a crown,
A field may till, or flock may feed.

This

This is one of the moft agreeable bafe fongs that I know. The melody is pleafing, and accompaniment ingenious and fpirited. And though the life of a mufical compofition is in general much fhorter than that of man, yet this bears its age fo well, that inftead of fifty-two years old, it feems in all the vigour and bloom of youth. It was compofed for Montagnano, one of the moft celebrated bafe fingers in HANDEL's fervice, when that fpecies of voice was more in fafhion, and perhaps more cultivated, than at prefent. The divifions require confiderable flexibility, and the compafs great extent of voice; both of which were well fupplied by Signor Tafca.

DUET, IN RODELINDA,
Compofed in 1725.

Madame MARA, and Signor BARTOLINI.

A 2.
> Io t'abbraccio;
> E più che morte
> Afpro e forte,
> E' pe'l cor mio
> Quefto addio
> Che il tuo fen dal mio divide.

Solo. *Ah mia vita!*

Sola. *Ah mio teforo!*

A 2.
> Se non moro,
> E' più tiranno
> Queft' affanno,
> Che da morte, e non uccide.

A 2.
> This laft embrace is worfe than death,
> Without the lofs of fenfe or breath;
> What torture to a faithful heart,
> From all that's dear, thus forc'd to part?

K

Sola.

Solo. My love!
Sola. My life!
Solo. My only hope!
Sola. My faithful wife!
A 2. { How barbarous is a tyrant's will,
      { Which death can give, yet does not kill!

The opening of modern Duets is generally more in Dialogue, and, perhaps, more dramatic, than was in fashion fifty or sixty years ago. Yet I am acquainted with no Duet upon the same model which pleases me more than this. It was introduced, with several of HANDEL's songs in a *pasticcio* Opera called *Lucio Vero*, in 1748; and I never was more delighted than with the performance of it, particularly where the composer, in the course of his modulation, has made such a happy use of the sharp seventh of each new key, enforced by the instruments, in a manner which was then totally new to my ears. There is not a passage, or point of imitation, in this Duet, which breathes not grace and dignity; and so far is the whole composition from discovering its age, that it seems of a kind which must be immortal, or at least an evergreen; which, however times and seasons vary, remains fresh and blooming as long as it exists.

XIth GRAND CONCERTO.

The first movement of this Concerto, though masterly, and built on a solid foundation, is uncommonly wild and capricious for the time when it was composed; the fugue is on a marked and active subject, which reminds us a little of some of our author's other instrumental fugues; but the symphony, or introduction, of the *andante*, is extremely pleasing; and no less remarkable for its grace, than the boldness with which the composer, in order to bring in the answers to points of imitation, has used

double

double difcords, *unprepared.* The Solo parts of this movement
were thought more brilliant, than eafy and natural to the bow and
finger-board, forty-years ago. Indeed the laft *Allegro,* which is
airy and fanciful, has Solo parts that feem more likely to have
prefented themfelves to the author at a harpfichord, than with a
violin in his hand; however, the whole Concerto was played in a
very chafte and fuperior manner, by Mr. Cramer; and it is but
juftice to this great performer to fay, that with a hand which de-
fies every poffible difficulty, he plays the productions of old
mafters with a reverential purity and fimplicity, that reflect
equal honour upon his judgment, good tafte, and underftanding.

AIR IN ALCINA,

Compofed in 1735.

Madame MARA.

Ah! mio cor! fchernito fei?
Stelle! Dei! nume d'amore?
Traditore! t'amo tanto,
Puoi lafciarmi fola in pianto?
Oh Dei! perche?
Ma che fà gemendo Alcina?
Son regina, e temo ancora?
Refti, o mora.
Pene fempre,
O torni a me.
Ah! mio cor! &c.

Alas! my heart! thou art now defpis'd!—
Ye pow'rs that move
Our hate and love,
Is this the way my paffion's priz'd?
Left by a wretch, whofe heart of fteel
Is dead to all I fay or feel.

K 2

But

But why let grief my foul devour?
I'm ftill a queen, and ftill have pow'r;
Which pow'r my vengeance foon fhall guide,
If ftill my kindnefs he deride.
Alas! my heart! &c.

This fong was always as much admired for its compofition, as Strada for her manner of finging it, when the Opera of Alcina firft appeared *(a)*. Perhaps a modern compofer, from the rage into which the enchantrefs is thrown in the Drama, by difcovering the intended departure of her favourite hero, Rogero, would have given the lady lefs tendernefs, and more paffion; however that may be, the firft ftrain of this Air, upon a continued moving bafe, is truly pathetic; and the conftant fobs and fighs, expreffed by fhort and broken notes in the violin and tenor parts, greatly add to this effect. Indeed, this movement contains fome ftrokes of modulation which are extremely bold and pathetic, particularly at the words *fola in pianto*. The fhort fecond part likewife expreffes much of the fpirit, agitation, and fury, which the words and fituation of the finger feem to require. If any one of the three furviving original performers in Alcina was prefent in the Pantheon during the performance of this Air, I cannot help fuppofing, that, in fpite of partiality for old times, and reverence for Strada, he, or fhe would have agreed with the reft of the audience, in greatly applauding madame Mara's manner of finging this impaffioned and difficult Air.

(a) Though near fifty years are elapfed fince, yet there are three of the original performers in that Drama ftill living: Mrs. Arne, widow of the late Dr. Arne, who was at that time a fcholar of Geminiani, and is called Mrs. Young, in the printed books; Mr. Savage, late fub-almoner, and vicar-choral of St. Paul's, who in the printed copy of the Mufic, is called *the boy*, and in the book of the words, *young Mr. Savage*; and Mr. Beard, fo long the favourite finger, and, afterwards, manager in one of our theatres.

ANTHEM.

A N T H E M.

Compofed for the Coronation of King GEORGE the Second, 1727.

" *My heart is inditing of a good matter* ; *I fpeak of the things*
" *which I have made unto the king.* Pf. xlv. 1.
" *Kings daughters were among thy honourable women.* Ibid. 10.
" *Upon thy right hand did ſtand the queen in veſture of gold* ;
" *and the king ſhall have pleaſure in thy beauty.* Ib. 12.
" *Kings ſhall be thy nurfing fathers, and queens thy nurfing*
" *mothers.*" Iſaiah xlix. 23.

This moſt pleaſing and admirable compoſition, the work of
HANDEL's youth and leiſure, contains ſo many peculiar beauties, that an enthuſiaſtic commentator might fill a conſiderable
volume in pointing them out. I ſhall try, however, in examining the ſcore, to moderate my admiration more than I was able
to do at its performance.

Of the firſt movement, the melody is remarkably well accented and pleaſing ; and the accompaniment clear, ingenious, and
maſterly. There is a dignity and ſobriety in the movement and
effect of the whole, well ſuited to compoſitions *à Capella* ; however, this is ſo much in HANDEL's *own* ſtyle, that no recollection
is awakened, either in the hearer or reader, of any other production, eccleſiaſtical or ſecular.

Indeed, nothing can exceed the ſeveral ſpecies of excellence
with which this movement is replete, except that which immediately follows it :

" *Kings daughters are among thy honourable women :*" which,
not only ſixty years ago was more original, but which ſtill re-

mains

mains unrivalled and uncommon.   Here a natural and beautiful melody is equally and artfully divided among the feveral principal voice-parts ; while the violin accompaniments, in a different ftyle of beautiful melody, are fo far from occafioning confufion, that they help to unite and cement the whole together.   The majeftic and regular movement of the bafe upon which fuch an admirable ftructure is built, muft ftrike judges of compofition with as much wonder, as uninftructed lovers of Mufic with delight.

The third movement, " *Upon thy right hand,*" &c. is as graceful in melody as rich in harmony ; and as new as if compofed but yefterday, except in one favourite paffage with HANDEL and his times, which being now a little *paffé*, is, perhaps, too often repeated for modern hearers *(a)*.

The fourth, and laft movement, " *Kings fhall be thy nurfing* " *fathers,*" is a full Chorus, big with all the fire, contrivance, rich harmony, and energy of genius, which HANDEL afterwards difplayed in his beft Oratorio Chorufes.   And this was the *finale* of the admirable mifcellaneous concert of *Commemoration* ; which if an exhibition of yet greater magnificence had not been given elfewhere, would have been ftill more admired, and worthy of celebrity.

(a) This is the paffage : which, in the courfe of the movement, occupies upwards of thirty bars.

THE DEAD SHALL LIVE. THE LIVING DIE.

HANDEL.

R.ᵗ SMIRK, Pinx.ᵗ

MAY 29 & MESSIAH. 1784.

Publiſh'd 29 May 1784.

COMMEMORATION

OF

HANDEL.

THIRD PERFORMANCE;

WESTMINSTER-ABBEY,

SATURDAY, May 29, 1784.

THE

MESSIAH.

THOUGH the company which attended this day's performance was confiderably more numerous thán that of Wednefday, yet, by the experience acquired, and meafures purfued,
fuch good order reigned in every department, that it was impoffible
to enter or quit a public place, of any kind, with more facility, or
to be feated more commodioufly, when there, than at this magnificent exhibition. And though the chief part of the audience,
by coming early, had a long period to fill up, yet, fuffering no inconvenience from numbers, heat, or cold; and having a building fo venerable, fo fitted up, and fo filled, to examine, all the languor, laffitude, and tedioufnefs were kept off, which ufually feiz?
both body and mind in public places, before the long expected pleafure arrives. The very filling the Abbey with fuch company, and
the Orcheftra with fuch performers, was a new, varied, and
amufing fpectacle, before the arrival of their Majefties and their
beautiful offspring crowned the whole, and rendered the *enfemble*
as enchanting to the eye, as fuch fublime Mufic, fo exquifitely
performed, muft have been to every ear.

L   PART

P A R T   I.

THE Overture to the MESSIAH, though grave and folemn, always feemed to me more dry and uninterefting in the performance, than the reft of HANDEL's Overtures; but the force, energy, and dignity, given to every trait of melody, as well as mafs of harmony, by this wonderful band, produced effects in it, which elude all defcription.

HANDEL's Overtures are generally analogous to the opening of the firft fcene of the Drama to which they belong, and may be called real prefaces or preliminary difcourfes to a book. In order therefore to fupprefs every idea of levity in fo facred a perform-ance as the MESSIAH, he very judicioufly finifhed the Overture without an Air. And the fhort fymphony to the accompanied Recitative, or *Aria parlante*, " *Comfort ye my people*," (Ifai. xl. 1.) feems to fuch as are not acquainted with the Oratorio, a preparation for the light minuet, gavot, or jig, with which Overtures are ufually terminated; but how exquifitely are judicious ears difappointed ! Indeed, I am acquainted with no movement of the fame caft, to the words of any language, which is more grateful and foothing than this. There is not a note, either in the principal melody or accompaniment, that is become vulgar, common, or unmean-ing. Mr. Harrifon, with his fweet and well-toned voice, did this Recitative and the following Air great juftice, by delivering
                                                                them

them with propriety and the utmoſt purity and truth of intonation *(a)*.

The Air, " *But who may abide the day of his coming,*" (Mal. iii. 2.)
is in a Sicilian paſtoral ſtyle, of which HANDEL was very fond,
and in which he was almoſt always ſuccefsful. And the Chorus:
" *And he ſhall purify the ſons of Levi,* is of a peculiar caſt: each
ſpecies of voice delivering the primitive ſubject, unaccompanied
by the reſt, till the counter-ſubject, in ligature, or binding-notes,
is introduced, which adds to the effect of the whole, when the
inſtruments come in, and all the voices, quitting the mazes of
fugue, unite in ſimple counterpoint.

There is a very curious expreſſion of the words attempted in
the Air: *The people who walked in darkneſs have ſeen a great light*;
(Iſai. ix. 2.) where the chromatic and indeterminate modulation,
ſeems to delineate the uncertain footſteps of perſons exploring their
way in obſcurity. Whether this imitation is obvious, or poſſible
to be made ſo, I know not; but there is merit in the attempt,
when it involves no abſurdity.

During the performance of this Oratorio, I made three ſeveral
pencil-marks, expreſſive of the degrees of comparative good with
which my ears were affected, by particular movements; and I
found the ſign of ſuperlative excellence ſtamped on the Chorus:

(a) HANDEL has certainly manifeſted great knowledge of the ſentiments and import of the words he had to expreſs in this Oratorio, though, when he ſet them, he was not perfectly acquainted with the pronunciation of our language: as, in the firſt Recitative, he has made a monoſyllable of *cryeth*; in the firſt Chorus frequently allows but one note to the word *Glory*; and in the ſecond Chorus of the ſecond part, he has made the word *ſurely* a triſyllable. This great maſter, with all his muſical riches and fertility of invention, was frequently obliged to be œconomical in his compoſitions as well as his affairs: and, when he was preſſed for time, he often applied words to Muſic, inſtead of Muſic to words; taking from its niche, or his port-folio, a movement already compoſed. Perhaps this was the caſe with the firſt Chorus: *The glory of the Lord*; which, however, is an excellent compoſition, and had a fine effect in the performance.

For

For unto us a child is born, (Ifai. ix. 6.) ; which has fo much merit of various kinds, that I know not where to begin to praife it. The fubjects of fugue are fo agreeable ; the violin accompaniments of fuch a peculiar character ; and the clearnefs and facility which reign through the whole fo uncommon, that each of them deferves to be particularly remarked ; but at every introduction of the words " *Wonderful! Counfellor! the mighty God! the everlafting Fa-* " *ther! the Prince of peace!*" which he fo long and fo judi- cioufly poftponed, the idea and effect are fo truly fublime, that, aflifted by the grandeur and energy of this band, I never felt the power of Choral Mufic and full harmony, in enforcing the ex- preflion of words, fo ftrongly before. There is poetry of the higheft clafs in the Mufic, as well as the words, of this Chorus.

The PASTORAL SYMPHONY which followed this *high- founding* Chorus, played without wind-inftruments by violins only, in the moft fubdued manner, was balmy and delicious ! The pianos or whifpers of fuch multiplied founds, produced a fweetnefs of fo new and exquifite a kind, that the mufical *technica* furnifhes no terms adequate to their effects.

R E C I T A T I V E.

" *There were fhepherds abiding in the field, keeping watch* " *over their flock by night.*" Luke ii. 8.

R E C I T A T I V E accompanied.

" *And, lo! an Angel of the Lord came upon them, and the glory* " *of the Lord fhone around them, and they were fore afraid.*" Matth. iii. 17. Luke ii. 9.

R E C I T A T I V E.

" *And the Angel faith unto them, Fear not ; for, behold! I* " *bring you good tidings of great joy, which fhall be to all people ;*

" *for*

" *for unto you is born this day, in the city of David, a Saviour,*
" *which is Chrift the Lord.*"   Luke ii. 10, 11.

RECITATIVE accompanied.

" *And fuddenly there was with the Angel a multitude of the*
" *Heavenly Hoft, praifing God, and faying.*"   Ibid. 13.

Thefe Recitatives, as delivered by the fweet voice and articulate pronunciation of Madame Mara, had an effect far beyond what might be expected from fuch few and fimple notes, without air, or meafure : they were literally made " *melting founds,*" to every hearer of fenfibility prefent. And the magnificent Chorus, " *Glory be* " *to God in the higheft! and peace on earth, good-will towards* " *men!*" (Ibid. 14.) in which the *pianos* and *fortes* were admirably marked and obferved, never had fo great an effect before, in any performance within my knowledge. There is more *claire obfcure* in this fhort Chorus than perhaps had ever been attempted at the time it was compofed. The anfwers to the fugue fucceeding each other fo clearly and clofely at the words " *good-will towards* " *men,*" muft always pleafe artifts, who know the ingenuity and merit of fuch contrivances ; but the general effects of this Chorus want nothing in the ignorant, but attention and feeling, to afford them unaccountable delight. " *Rejoice greatly, O daughter* " *of Zion; fhout! O daughter of Jerufalem; behold! thy king* " *cometh unto thee.*   Zechariah ix. 9.

" *He is the righteous Saviour, and he fhall fpeak peace unto the* " *Heathen.*"   Ibid. 10.

This brilliant and difficult Air afforded Madame Mara an opportunity of difplaying fome of her wonderful powers of execution, and fhewed her in a very different light from any thing fhe

had

had hitherto fung at the Commemoration ; but fo firm, fweet, and judicious, was her performance of every kind, and fo delight- ful to the audience, that fhe never breathed a found without effect.

" *He fhall feed his flock like a fhepherd*," (Ifai. xl. 11.) is an Air in HANDEL's beft *Siciliana* ftyle, and has ever been in great favour with performers and hearers : Guadagni, after Mrs. Cibber, efta- blifhed its reputation.   It is fimilar in movement to the lulling paftoral at the end of Corelli's Eighth Concerto, " *Fatto per la* " *notte di natale*," and had a pleafing effect from the performance of Signor Bartolini, and Mifs Cantelo.

PART

P A R T   II.

THE Second Part of this divine Oratorio abounds in fo many beauties of compofition and effect, that I find one of my three marks affixed to almoft every movement. The Chorus, " *Behold the Lamb of God, that taketh away the fins of the* " *world,*" (St. John i. 29.) has the fingle ftamp of folemnity ; but the Air, " *He was defpifed and rejected of men,*" (Ifai. liii. 3.) has ever impreffed me with the higheft idea of excellence in pathetic expreffion, of any Englifh fong with which I am acquainted. " *Surely* " *he hath borne our griefs,*" (Ibid. l. 4, 5.) is an admirable piece of learned counterpoint and modulation, and very expreffive of the words. The fubfequent *alla breve* fugue, to the words " *And with* " *his ftripes we are healed,*" is written upon a fine fubject, with fuch clearnefs and regularity as was never furpaffed by the greateft Choral compofers of the fixteenth century. This fugue, which is purely vocal, and *à Capella,* as the inftruments have no other bufinefs affigned them than that of doubling and enforcing the voice-parts, may fairly be compared with movements of the fame kind in Paleftrina, Tallis, and Bird, which, in variety, it very much furpaffes.

C H O R U S.

" *All we, like fheep, have gone aftray ; we have turned every* " *one to his own way.*" Ifai. liii. 6.

This Chorus has a fpirit, and beauties of compofition, of a quite different kind : the bafe is *coftretto,* and moving inceffantly in

quavers

quavers, while the voice-parts and violins expreſs a roving, care-
leſs kind of paſtoral wildneſs, which is very characteriſtic of the
words. " *And the Lord hath laid on him the iniquity of us all.*"
Iſai. liii. 6.   This fragment is full of ſorrow and contrition.

The words of the admirable choral fugue: " *He truſted in*
" *God that he would deliver him ; let him deliver him, if he delight*
" *in him,*" (Matth. xxvii. 43. and Pſal. xxii. 8.) which contain
the triumphal inſolence, and are prophetic of the contumelious language of the Jews, during the crucifixion of our Saviour, were very
difficult to expreſs ; however, HANDEL, availing himſelf in the
moſt maſterly manner of the advantage of fugue and imitation,
has given them the effect, not of the taunts and preſumption of
an individual, but the ſcoffs and ſcorn of a confuſed multitude *(a)*.

" *Thy rebuke hath broken his heart ; he is full of heavineſs : he*
" *looked for ſome to have pity on him, but there was no man, neither*
" *found he any to comfort him.*" (Pſal. lxix. 21.)   This is a piece
of accompanied Recitative of the pathetic kind, no leſs honourable
to the Compoſer's feeling, than muſical learning and recondite modulation : and all the ſorrowful caſt and expreſſion of that and the
Air which follows it : " *Behold and ſee, if there be any ſorrow*
" *like unto his ſorrow !*" (Lam. of Jeremiah, i. 12.) were well
preſerved by the performance of Mr. Norris.

The happy conſtruction of Weſtminſter-Abbey for cheriſhing
and preſerving muſical tones, by a gentle augmentation without
echo or repetition, was demonſtrated by no part of the performance more clearly than in that of Miſs Abrams ; whoſe voice,

(a) He was ſo conſcious of the merit of
this movement, that he frequently performed it on key'd-inſtruments, as a leſſon ; and
if he was preſſed to ſit down to play at ſuch
times as he felt no immediate impulſe, this
theme uſually preſented itſelf to his mind ;
when, making it the ſubject of extempore
fugue and voluntary, it never failed to in-
ſpire him with the moſt ſublime ideas, and
wonderful ſallies of imagination.

though

though sweet and of a good quality, is not regarded as Theatrical, but such as the Italians denominate *Voce di Camera*. Yet, in singing the pleasing Air, " *But thou didst not leave his soul in hell,*" (Psf. xvi. 11.) which she did with considerable taste and expression, her voice was rendered more audible in every part of that immense building, than it has ever been in any Concert-Room in London.

CHORUS.

" *Lift up your heads, O ye gates, and be ye lift up, ye everlast-*
" *ing doors, and the King of Glory shall come in !*" Psal. xxiv. 7.

SEMI-CHORUS.

" *Who is this King of Glory ?*

SEMI-CHORUS.

" *The Lord strong and mighty, the Lord mighty in battle.*

SEMI-CHORUS.

" *Lift up your heads, O ye gates, and be ye lift up, ye everlast-*
" *ing doors, and the King of Glory shall come in !*

SEMI-CHORUS.

" *Who is this King of Glory ?*

SEMI-CHORUS.

" *The Lord of Hosts ; he is the King of Glory.*

CHORUS.

" *The Lord of Hosts ; he is the King of Glory.*"

All these words are admirably expressed, and the contrasted effects of Semi-Chorus and Chorus, were never more striking than in the performance of to-day.

M

CHORUS.

" Let all the Angels of God worſhip him." Heb. i. 6.

This ſpirited fugue, ſeemingly on two ſubjects, is, perhaps, the moſt artificial that has been compoſed in modern times. HANDEL, in order to exerciſe his abilities in every ſpecies of difficulty which the moſt learned and elaborate Canoniſts and Fughiſts of the fifteenth and ſixteenth centuries were ambitious of vanquiſhing, has compoſed this movement in what ancient theoriſts called *minor Prolation*; in which the reply to a ſubject given, though in ſimilar intervals, is made in notes of different value: as when the theme is led off in ſemibreves and anſwered in minims, or the contrary *(a)*.

" The Lord gave the word; great was the company of the preachers." Pſal. lxvii. 11.

The majeſty and dignity of the few ſolemn notes with which this Chorus is begun, without inſtruments, received great augmentation now, from being delivered by ſuch a number of baſe and tenor voices in uniſon; and the contraſt of ſenſation occaſioned by the harmony and activity of the ſeveral parts, afterwards, had a very ſtriking effect.

" How beautiful are the feet of them that preach the goſpel of " peace, and bring glad tidings of good things!" (Iſai. lii. 7. and Rom. x. 15.) is a very pleaſing Air, *alla Siciliana*, which Signor Bartolini

---

(a) As it is only profeſſors who can eſtimate the difficulty of finding a ſubject which will ſerve as an accompaniment to itſelf in notes of augmentation or diminution, it is to them that the examination of this Chorus is recommended, who will ſee that while one part is performing the theme in crotchets and quavers, another is conſtantly repeating it in quavers and ſemiquavers: an exerciſe for ingenuity often practiſed about two hundred years ago, on a few ſlow notes, or in fragments of canto fermo; but never before, I believe, in ſo many parts, with ſuch perfect airy freedom, or little appearance of reſtraint and difficulty.

ſung

fung with elegant fimplicity. And " *their found is gone out*," (Pf. xix. 4.) and " *Let us break their bonds afunder*," (Pf. ii. 3.) both upon two different fubjects, are capital Chorufes in very different ftyles, as well as meafure, and were performed with the utmoft fpirit and precifion; but I haften to fpeak of the Allelujah, which is the triumph of HANDEL, of the COMMEMORATION, and of the mufical art.

The opening is clear, chearful, and bold. And the words, " *For the Lord God omnipotent reigneth*," (Rev. xix. 6.) fet to a fragment of canto fermo, which all the parts fing, as fuch, in uni-fons and octaves, has an effect truly ecclefiaftical. It is afterwards made the fubject of fugue and ground-work for the Allelujah. Then, as a fhort epifode in plain counter-point, we have " *The* " *kingdom of this world*" (Ib. ix. 15.)—which being begun *piano*, was folemn and affecting. But the laft and principal fubject pro-pofed, and led off by the bafe—" *And he fhall reign for ever and* " *ever*," is the moft pleafing and fertile that has ever been invented fince the art of fugue was firft cultivated. It is marked, and con-ftantly to be diftinguifhed through all the parts, accompaniments, counter-fubjects and contrivances, with which it is charged. And, finally, the words—" *King of Kings, and Lord of Lords*, (Ib. xix. 16.) always fet to a fingle found, which feems to ftand at bay, while the other parts attack it in every poffible manner, in " *Alle-* " *lujahs—for ever and ever*," is a moft happy and marvellous con-catination of harmony, melody, and great effects.

Dante, in his *Paradifo*, imagines nine circles, or choirs of che-rubs, feraphs, patriarchs, prophets, martyrs, faints, angels, and archangels, who with hand and voice are eternally praifing and glo-rifying the Supreme Being, whom he places in the centre; taking the idea from *Te Deum laudamus*, where it is faid : " *To thee Che-*

rubim

rubim and Seraphim continually do cry," &c. Now as the Orcheſtra in Weſtminſter Abbey, ſeemed to aſcend into the clouds and unite with the ſaints and martyrs repreſented on the painted glaſs in the weſt window, which had all the appearance of a continuation of the Orcheſtra; I could hardly refrain, during the performance of the Allelujah, to imagine that this Orcheſtra, ſo admirably conſtructed, filled, and employed, was a point or ſegment of one of theſe celeſtial circles. And perhaps, no band of mortal muſicians ever exhibited a more reſpectable appearance to the eye, or afforded a more extatic and affecting ſound to the ear, than this.

" So ſung they, and the empyrèan rung
" With Allelujahs."

PART

P A R T   III.

" *I Know that my Redeemer liveth, and that he will stand at* " *the latter day upon the earth: and though worms destroy* " *this body, yet in my flesh I shall see God.* (Job xix. 25, 26.) " *For now is Christ risen from the dead, the first fruits of them* *that sleep.*" 1 Cor. xv. 20.

It has been said, I think, inconsiderately, " that the Airs of " the MESSIAH are greatly inferior to most of those in HANDEL's " Operas, and other Oratorios." It would not, however, be difficult to point out eight or ten Airs of peculiar merit in this Oratorio; among which, " *Every Valley*"—preceded by the accompanied Recitative, " *Comfort ye my people*"—*He shall feed his* " *flock*—*He was despised*—and *I know that my Redeemer liveth*"— are so excellent, that it would not be easy to find their equals in any one of his Operas or other Oratorios. Indeed, the universal rapture visible in the countenances of this uncommonly numerous and splendid audience, during the whole time that madame Mara was performing the very affecting Air with which the IIId part of the MESSIAH is opened : " *I know that my Redeemer liveth*," exceeded every silent expression of delight from Music which I had ever before observed. Her power over the sensibility of the audience seemed equal to that of Mrs. Siddons. There was no eye within my view which did not

——— " silently a gentle tear let fall."

Nor

Nor, though long hackneyed in Mufic, did I find myfelf made

" of ftronger earth than others."

At the end of her performance of this Air, the audience feemed
burfting with applaufe for which the place allowed of no decorous
means of utterance. The Italians, when much pleafed with
Mufic in their churches, manifeft rapture by coughing, fpitting,
blowing their nofes, or fcraping their feet, which with us are
expreffions of contempt. The conftruction, however, of thefe
audible figns are eafy and intelligible, when once they are fettled
by national compact.

After this juftly admired Air, the fhort Semi-chorus: " *Since*
" *by man came death,*" in plain counterpoint, by the principal
foprano, counter-tenor, tenor, and bafe, without inftruments,
had a fweet and folemn effect, which heightened the beauty of the
following Chorus: " *By man came alfo the refurrection of the*
dead." And the Semi-chorus, " *for as in Adam all die,*" fung
in the fame unaccompanied manner, by three of the beft fingers
in each of the four fpecies of voice, contrafted admirably with the
full Chorus—" *Even fo in Chrift fhall all be made alive.*"

The effect of contraft in thefe movements, alternately fung
with, and without inftruments, was fo agreeable and ftriking,
that it were to be wifhed more frequent ufe was made of fuch an
eafy expedient.

The favourite Bafe fong, " *The Trumpet fhall found,*" (1 Cor. xv.
52.) was very well performed by Signor Tafca and Mr. Sarjant, who
accompanied him on the trumpet admirably. There are, however,
fome paffages in the trumpet-part to this Air, which have always
a bad effect, from the natural imperfection of the inftrument. In
HANDEL's time, compofers were not fo delicate in writing for

Trumpets

Trumpets and French-horns, as at prefent; it being now laid down as a rule, that the fourth and fixth of a key on both thefe inftruments, being *naturally* fo much out of tune that no player can make them perfect, fhould never be ufed but in fhort paffing notes, to which no bafe is given that can difcover their falfe intonation.   Mr. Sarjeant's tone is extremely fweet and clear, but every time that he was obliged to dwell upon G, the fourth of D, difpleafure appeared in every countenance; for which I was extremely concerned, knowing how inevitable fuch an effect muft be from fuch a caufe *(a)*.

The Chorus—" *But thanks be to God,*" (Ibid. 57.) and the Air—" *If God is for us,*" Rom. viii. 31), fung by Mifs Cantelo, were well performed, and had very pleafing effects.

" *Worthy is the Lamb that was flain, and hath redeemed us to*
" *God by his blood, to receive power, and riches, and wifdom, and*
" *ftrength, and honour, and glory, and bleffing.* Rev. v. 12.

" *Bleffing and honour, glory and power, be unto Him that fit-*
" *teth upon the throne, and unto the Lamb, for ever and ever!*
" *Amen.*" Ibid. 13.

Of thefe three final Chorufes it is difficult to determine which is the beft, or had the grandeft effect, from the very uncommon force and accuracy with which they were now performed.   But though thefe three admirable movements are all in the fame key and meafure, yet their characters are totally different: the firft—
" *Worthy is the Lamb*—in folemn, fimple counterpoint, and

(a) In the Allelujah, p. 150, of the printed fcore, G, the fourth of the key, is founded and fuftained during two entire bars. In the Dettingen *Te Deum*, p. 30, and in many other places, this *falfe concord*, or interval, perpetually deforms the fair face of harmony, and indeed the face of almoft every one that hears it, with an expreffion of pain. It is very much to be wifhed that this animating and brilliant inftrument could have its defects removed by fome ingenious mechanical contrivance, as thofe of the German flute are, by keys.

modu-

modulation, is flow; with alternate ſtrains of an accelerated movement, to which there is a very ingenious and pleaſing accompaniment for the violins, totally different from the voice-parts.

" *Bleſſing and honour, glory and power (a), be unto him that* " *ſitteth upon the throne, and unto the Lamb, for ever and ever.*"

This ſecond Chorus on a marked, ſpirited, and pleaſing ſubject of fugue, in the ſtyle of canto fermo, is led off by the tenors aud baſes, in uniſon; then it is repeated by the trebles an octave higher, without accompaniments, till the point :—" *that ſitteth* " *upon the throne,*" is anſwered by the tenors. After which the counter-tenors introduce the firſt ſubject, and are followed by the baſes. When all the parts have ſung the whole ſubject, which is long, particular ſections of it are made points of imitation. And after the fugue has been well treated in all the relative keys,

while

(a) The ſeeming contraction of the words in the notation of this paſſage, has a barbarous appearance to the eye: as HANDEL has allowed but three notes to five ſyllables; though the time is ſo ſlow (*Larghetto*) that no eliſion in ſinging them ſeems neceſſary. *e. g.*

Bleſſing and honour, glory and

power, be un-to him, &c.

The compoſer, from the little experience he had had in ſetting Engliſh words, in the year 1741, thinking the rapid manner in which the language is pronounced in converſation ſhould be followed in reading and ſinging poetry and lofty proſe, ſet the words of this Chorus thus :

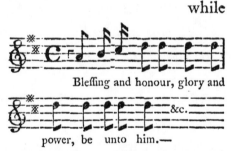

Bleſſing and honour, glory and

power, be unto him.—

and this notation has been literally followed in all tranſcripts and editions of the Oratorio ever ſince.

This little defect would certainly not have been pointed out here, had it not been with the wiſh of indicating an apology for it, and a cure. In future editions and tranſcripts of ſo claſſical a production, it ſeems neceſſary to recommend the correction of this and a few other ſimilar inaccuracies, leſt mere verbal critics, laying too much ſtreſs on ſuch trivial defects, ſhould endeavour to diminiſh the glory of the author and his work while the violins are moving in femi-quavers, the important words " *bleffing, honour, glory,*"—are diftinctly and judicioufly pronounced by all the vocal parts together, in plain counter-point, with a crotchet reft, or mufical comma, between each of them. Then, with a fire, fpirit, and refources peculiar to HAN-DEL, this admirable Chorus is wound up with reiterations of the words " *for ever and ever,*" in all the fplendor of full har-mony and animated movement.

And, at length, when thofe who hear the MESSIAH for the firft time imagine the whole performance to be completely and glorioufly finifhed, *a finale* is led off by the bafes, in a fugue, upon a noble fubject, to the Hebrew conclufive term of devotion, *Amen.* In the courfe of this movement the fubject is divided, fubdivided, inverted, enriched with counter-fubjects, and made fubfervient to many ingenious and latent purpofes of harmony, melody, and imitation; with the effects of which, though all muft be ftruck and delighted, yet thofe only are able to comprehend the whole merit of contexture in this Chorus, who have ftudied har-mony or counter-point, and are capable of judging of defign, ar-rangement, contrivance, and all the ingenious mazes and perplexities of elaborate compofitions. Here HANDEL, unembarraffed by words, gave a loofe to genius, liberated from all reftraints but thofe of his own art. An inftrumental fugue could not be more free and unconfined than this, upon an open vowel, and a fyl-lable that terminates with the eafy appulfe of the tongue and teeth, which the liquid letter *n* requires. Symphonies of a fo-lemn kind, without finging, are frequently played in the Italian

work. And, indeed, however flight or un-important fuch overfights may be to lovers of Mufic, to mere grammarians and philo-logers, they appear unpardonable.

N churches,

churches, during the *Meſſa baſſa*, or ſilent celebration of the maſs. And diviſions on particular words and ſyllables, which are thought innovations and modern fopperies, have been proved of the higheſt antiquity in the church, and the authority of Saint Auguſtine has been cited in apology for their uſe *(a)*.

(a) " When we are unable to find words " worthy of the Divinity, we do well, ſays " this ſaint, to addreſs him with confuſed " ſounds of joy and thankſgiving. For " to whom are ſuch extatic ſounds due, un- " leſs to the Supreme Being ? And how " can we celebrate his ineffable goodneſs, " when we are equally unable to adore him " in ſilence, and to find any other expreſ- " ſions of our tranſports, than inarticulate " ſounds ?" *Hiſtory of Muſic*, vol. ii. p. 172.

COM-

Pl. VI.

E.F.Burney del.   J.Spilsbury

View of the Gallery prepared for the reception of their Majesties, the Royal Family, Directors, & principal Personages in the Kingdom, at the **COMMEMORATION** *of* **HANDEL** *in Westminster Abbey.*

COMMEMORATION

OF

HANDEL.

FOURTH PERFORMANCE,

WESTMINSTER-ABBEY.

June 3, 1784.

BY COMMAND OF HIS MAJESTY.

[To face P. 91.]

Selection of Sacred Music for the Fourth Commemoration
Performance.

PART I.

OVERTURE—ESTHER.
The Dettingen TE DEUM.

PART II.

OVERTURE OF TAMERLANE, and Dead March in SAUL.
Part of the FUNERAL ANTHEM.
When the ear heard him.
He delivered the poor that cried.
His body is buried in peace.
GLORIA PATRI, from the JUBILATE.

PART III.

AIR AND CHORUS—*Jehovah crown'd with glory bright.*
In ESTHER.
FIRST GRAND CONCERTO.
CHORUS—*Gird on thy sword.* In SAUL.
FOURTH HAUTBOIS CONCERTO.
ANTHEM—*O sing unto the Lord all the whole earth.*
CHORUS—*The Lord shall reign for ever and ever.* ISRAEL
IN EGYPT.
CORONATION ANTHEM. *Zadoc the Priest.*

INTRODUCTION.

THE preceding performances having given such entire satisfaction to all that were present, and becoming, of course, the general subject of discussion and praise, excited a great desire in all lovers of Music, and even of splendid spectacles, who were absent, to be enabled to judge and speak of transactions so memorable, from the conviction of their own senses. But even these were not more eager in wishing there might be a repetition of the performances, than those who had already attended them. Luckily for all parties, the wishes of their Majesties coincided with those of their subjects; and as the scaffolding was still standing, and the band not yet dispersed, two more opportunities were given for the display of HANDEL's wonderful powers, and the gratification of public curiosity.

On Monday, the last day of May, these two additional performances had the advantage of being announced in the public papers, with the most honourable and indubitable testimony of Royal Patronage, in the following manner.

BY

" By COMMAND of His MAJESTY.

In Commemoration of HANDEL, under the Direction of the

Earl of Exeter	Sir Watkin Williams Wynn,
Earl of Sandwich	Bart.
Earl of Uxbridge	Sir Richard Jebb, Bart.

On THURSDAY next, the 3d of June, there will be an additional performance of

S A C R E D   M U S I C,

In Weftminfter-Abbey,

Confifting of the following Pieces compofed by that Great Mafter.

P A R T   I.

Overture, Efther.

The Dettingen Te Deum.

P A R T   II.

Overture, Tamerlane—with the Dead March in Saul.

When the Ear heard him,

He delivered the Poor that cried, } From the Funeral Anthem.

His Body is buried in Peace,

Gloria Patri, from the Jubilate.

P A R T   III.

Firft Grand Concerto.

Chorus.—Gird on thy Sword, from Saul.

Fourth Hautboy Concerto.

Anthem.—O fing unto the Lord all the whole Earth.

Chorus—The Lord fhall reign for ever and ever, from Ifrael in Egypt.

Coronation Anthem.—Zadock the Prieft.

The doors will be opened at Nine o'Clock precifely, and the performance will begin at Twelve, when the doors will be fhut.

Tickets for this Performance will be delivered at One Guinea each, at the St. Alban's Tavern, in St. Alban's-ftreet, and no where elfe, on Tuefday the 1ft, and Wednefday the 2d of June, between the hours of Ten in the morning, and Ten in the evening of each day, and after that time no Tickets can be delivered, or Money taken; but when the number of Tickets fhall be judged fufficient to fill the places allotted for the company, the delivery of them will be ftopped before the hour of Ten on Wednefday night.

The profits arifing from this performance, as well as thofe of the former ones, will be applied to charitable purpofes."

" By COMMAND of Her MAJESTY.
On Saturday next, June 5, being the LAST DAY of the
COMMEMORATION OF HANDEL,
Will be performed in Weftminfter-Abbey,
Under the Management of the

Earl of Exeter	Sir Watkin Williams Wynn,
Earl of Sandwich	Bart.
Earl of Uxbridge	Sir Richard Jebb, Bart.

The SACRED ORATORIO of
T H E   M E S S I A H.

The doors will be opened at Nine o'Clock precifely, and the performance will begin at Twelve, when the doors will be fhut.

Tickets to be had at the St. Alban's Tavern, on Friday next, and no where elfe, from Eight in the Morning, till Ten at Night.

The profits arifing from this performance, as well as thofe of the former ones, will be applied to charitable purpofes."

Experience is fuch an admirable inftructrefs, that every little perplexity, or unexpected embarraffment, which had occafioned the leaft trouble or inconvenience to the company, in approaching or entering the Abbey, had been fo entirely removed by the well-concerted meafures which the Directors and their affiftants had taken, that no affemblies equally numerous were, perhaps, ever formed before, on any occafion, with fuch perfect facility as thefe.

Though the pieces performed in the Abbey, on the firft Day of Commemoration, were fo admirably executed, and univerfally approved, yet as there were a few changes and additions to be made at the particular inftance of his Majefty, a public rehearfal was advertifed for Wednefday, at which upwards of Eight hundred perfons were prefent, who paying half guineas for admiffion, confiderably augmented the clear profits appropriated to charitable purpofes.

The order in which the feveral pieces of this day were performed, is the following:

PART

PART I.

OVERTURE IN ESTHER. 1722.

THE DETTINGEN TE DEUM. 1743.

OF thefe excellent productions, nothing need be added to what has already been faid, in the account of the firft day's performance *(a)*; except, that for accuracy of execution, and grandeur of effect, they now merited ftill warmer praife.

(a) See p. 27, 28.

PART

P A R T   II.

O V E R T U R E   I N   T A M E R L A N E.
Compofed 1724.
WITH THE DEAD MARCH IN SAUL,
1740.

When the ear heard him, &c.　　　⎫　Funeral Anthem.
He delivered the poor that cried, &c.　⎬
His body is buried in peace, &c.　　⎭　Compofed 1737.
Gloria Patri　　-　　-　　-　　*Jubilate* 1713.

THE only change that was made in the pieces of this part
of to-day's performance, was playing the two firft movements of the Overture in *Tamerlane*, inftead of the firft movement of the Overture in *Saul*, which was very judicious, and
produced an admirable effect.　The opening of the Overture in
Tamerlane is remarkably majeftic in itfelf; and the powerful
manner in which all the parts were this day enforced, augmented
its dignity and importance.　The fugue, upon a marked, lively,
and airy fubject, is fo clofely and ingenioufly worked, as to be
continually heard in one or other of the parts; for even where
the hautbois are left to themfelves, the folo paffages allotted to
them arife either out of the fubject of the movement, or its in-
verfion.　It was wonderfully compact in performance, and after
being twice played with the precifion of a few felect hands, and
the effect of myriads; from its being in a minor key, and in an
animated movement, it contributed much to brighten the grateful richnefs of the harmony, as well as to give dignity to the flow
and folemn meafure, of the

DEAD MARCH IN SAUL.

PART III.

AIR AND CHORUS IN ESTHER.

Compoſed in 1720 *(a)*.

AIR.

Jehovah crown'd with glory bright,
Surrounded with eternal light,
Whoſe miniſters are flames of fire,
Ariſe, and execute thine ire (b).

CHORUS.

He comes, he comes, to end our woes,
And pour his vengeance on our foes.
Earth trembles, lofty mountains nod,
Jacob ariſe, to meet thy God
He comes, &c. (c).

(a) Though this Oratorio was compoſed ſo early as 1720, for the duke of Chandos, at Cannons, yet it was not publickly performed till May, 1732; when it ran during ten nights.

(b This Air is more than an imitation of the following lines in the laſt Chorus of the 2d Act of Racine's Eſther.

> *O Dieu, que la gloire couronne!*
> *Dieu, que la lumiere environne!*
> *Qui voles ſur l'aile des vent,——*
> *Donne à ton nom la victoire.*

(c) Arme-toi, vien nous defendre.
Deſcends tel qu'autrefois la Mer te vit deſcendre.
Que les mechans apprennent aujourd'hui
A craindre ta colere.

I never could aſcertain who was the writer of this Oratorio, in Engliſh: according to the author of the *Bibl. Brit. Tom.* xv. 1740, it was aſcribed to Pope and Arbuthnot; but, by whomſoever it was produced, there is certainly ſomething in many of the lines that ſeems entitled to the name of poetry.

The

The invocation to the Divinity in the Air, as well as his an-
nunciation in the fubfequent Chorus, are fet in a ftyle fo peculiarly grand, that they ought not to be paffed by without fomething more than an indifcriminate acknowledgment of their excellence.

The opening of this fcene in the firft Sacred Drama that was
fet to Mufic by HANDEL, bears all the marks of a grand and
fublime genius. He was now arrived at the age of thirty-fix,
when, after writing for the firft performers in Europe, vocal and
inftrumental, his judgment was matured fufficiently to guide,
without abating his fire and enthufiafm. And this Chorus feems
entitled to admiration for a different fpecies of merit from
the generality of his Oratorio Chorufes, to which we liften with
wonder, at the knowledge, contrivance, art of fugue, or richnefs of harmony with which they abound; for this has all the
fpirit and activity of a compofition truly *dramatic*. And the perpetual agitation of the inftrumental parts helps the expreffion of
the words, in a moft wonderful manner.

Indeed the accompaniments are fo full and complete, that they
feem to have been written before the voice-parts, which are chiefly
in plain counterpoint; furnifhing fuch fimple fundamental harmony as the right-hand of a harpfichord-player might comprefs
into chords, in accompanying the bafe. There is neither fugue
nor imitation carried on in this Chorus, except for a few bars, at
the words, " *to end our woes—And pour his vengeance on our*
" *foes.*"—But at the fecond ftrain—" *Earth trembles,*" &c.
there is a grandeur of expreffion and effect, which, as it was the
firft time I had ever heard this compofition performed, acted on
my feelings in a very uncommon manner.

O 2 As

As fome of my readers may, perhaps, wifh to know a few circumftances belonging to the hiftory of this *primitive* Oratorio,
befides thofe that have been related in the Life of HANDEL,
p. 22 ; the following information has been obtained from Dr. Randal, the mufical profeffor at Cambridge, and Mr. Barrow, who were
among the original performers, when it was dramatically reprefented.

On the firft performance of ESTHER, in action, at the houfe
of Mr. Bernard Gates, Mafter of the Children of the Chapel-
Royal, in 1731, the parts were caft in the following manner:

Efther - -	by Mr. John (now Dr.) Randal.
Affuerus, and firft Ifraelite -	James Butler.
Haman - - -	John Moore.
Mordecai, and Ifraelite Boy -	John Brown.
Prieft of the Ifraelites - -	John Beard.
Harbonah - - - -	Price Clevely.
Perfian Officer, and 2d Ifraelite	James Allen.
Ifraelites }	Samuel (late Dr.) Howard.
and } - -	Mr. Thomas Barrow.
Officers }	Robert Denham.

Soon after this, it was twice performed by the fame children,
at the Crown and Anchor, by the defire of William Huggins,
efq. a member of that Society, and tranflator of Ariofto, publifhed 1757, who furnifhed the dreffes. Mr. HANDEL himfelf
was prefent at one of thefe reprefentations, and having mentioned
it to the Princefs Royal, his illuftrious fcholar, her Royal Highnefs was pleafed to exprefs a defire to fee it exhibited in action at
the Opera-houfe in the Hay-market, by the fame young performers ; but Dr. Gibfon, then bifhop of London, would not grant
permiffion for its being reprefented on that ftage, even with books

in

in the children's hands. Mr. HANDEL, however, the next year, had it performed at that theatre, with additions to the Drama, by Humphreys; but in *ftill life:* that is, without action, in the fame manner as Oratorios have been fince conftantly performed. The Drama exhibited by the children confifted only of two acts: beginning with the Recitative, " *Tis greater far,*" &c. as it had been originally fet for the duke of Chandos.

The firft Oratorios that were performed in Italy, at the beginning of the laft century, were *facred Dramas,* or *Reprefentations,* performed in action; and *Efther* and *Athalie* were exhibited in France, at the convent of St. Cyr, in that manner. It feems to have been a cuftom of very ancient ftanding, for our court to employ the children of the chapel in dramatic reprefentations, under the direction of the mafter of the revels. And in the houfhold book of the earls of Northumberland, it appears that the fame ufe was originally made of the finging-boys of their domeftic chapel. It appears likewife that moft of Ben Jonfon's Mafques, written for queen Elizabeth and king James the Firft, were acted and fung by the children of the Chapel-Royal; and among his Epigrams, we find an epitaph on S. P. a child of queen Elizabeth's chapel, whofe talents for acting are more celebrated than thofe for finging *(a)*.

(a) " Weep with me all you that read
   This little ftory:
And know for whom a tear you fhed,
   Death's felf is forry.
'Twas a child that fo did thrive
   In grace and feature,
As heav'n and nature feem'd to ftrive
   Which own'd the creature.
Yeares he number'd fcarce thirteen
   When *Fates* turn'd cruel,
Yet three fill'd zodiackes had he been
   The ftages jewel;

And did act, what now we moane
   Old men fo duely,
As footh the *Parcæ* thought him one,
   He play'd fo truely.
So by error to his fate
   They all confented;
But viewing him fince, alas too late,
   They have repented;
And have fought to give new birth,
   In bathes to fteep him;
But, being fo much too good for earth,
   Heav'n vows to keep him."
   Ben Jonfon's Works, Fol. Edit. p. 38.

FIRST

FIRST GRAND CONCERTO.

If the epithet *grand*, inftead of implying, as it ufually does, many parts, or a Concerto requiring a great band or Orcheftra, had been here intended to exprefs fublimity and dignity, it might have been ufed with the utmoft propriety; for I can recollect no movement that is more lofty and noble than this; or in which the treble and bafe of the *tutti*, or full parts, are of two fuch diftinct and marked characters; both bold, and contrafted, not only with each other, but with the folo parts, which are graceful and *chantant*. Nor did I ever know fo much bufinefs done in fo fhort a time; that movement contains but thirty-four bars, and yet nothing feems left unfaid; and though it begins with fo much pride and haughtinefs, it melts, at laft, into foftnefs; and, where it modulates into a minor key, feems to exprefs fatigue, languor, and fainting.

The fubject of the next movement is gay and pleafing. And, when the firft violin has a feries of iterated notes, in fcale, by thirds with the bafe, the fecond violin renders them interefting by the poignancy of fharp fifths, mounting up to fixths, ufed as *appoggiaturas*, or notes of tafte. In the *adagio*, while the two trebles are finging in the ftyle of vocal duets of the time, where thefe parts, though not in regular fugue, abound in *imitations* of the fugue kind; the bafe, with a boldnefs and character peculiar to HANDEL, fupports with learning and ingenuity the fubject of the two firft bars, either direct or inverted, throughout the movement, in a clear, diftinct, and marked manner. The fugue upon an airy pleafing theme, is clofely worked and carried on from the beginning to the end without epifode, or divi-

fion

fion foreign to the fubject, and in a modulation ftrictly confined to the key note and its fifth : thofe who know the merit and difficulty of this fpecies of compofition can alone be fenfible of our author's refources and fuperiority, whenever fugue is in queftion. The laft *Allegro*, in the time of a quick Minuet, contains many graceful and pleafing paffages, particularly in the folo parts. I have often heard this Concerto well performed at Vaux-hall, Ranelagh, and other places, foon after its publication, by what were, then, thought *great bands*; but the force, dignity, and importance given to every paffage and combination by this unparalleled band, renovated and furpaffed all the pleafure it ever afforded me before.

CHORUS IN SAUL.

Compofed 1740.

Gird on thy fword, thou man of might,
Purfue thy wonted fame ;
Go on, be profperous in fight,
Retrieve the Hebrew name.

Thy ftrong right hand with terror arm'd,
Shall thy obdurate foes difmay ;
While others, by thy virtue charm'd,
Shall crowd to own thy righteous fway.

This Chorus is extremely animating and fpirited ; and, as the words imply, being intended to roufe and ftimulate a hero to take the field, feemed, in the performance by fo numerous a band, to exprefs the clamorous entreaties of a whole people. The point " *retrieve the Hebrew name,*" led off in the middle of this

Chorus,

Chorus, contrasted admirably with the artful and intentional confusion of the beginning; and the artless simplicity of the last movement,—" *while others by thy virtue charmed*," led off in a kind of *canto fermo*, by upwards of sixty tenor voices, in unison, had an effect to which our ears are wholly unaccustomed. Indeed, the powerful manner in which this subject was delivered, singly, by the other parts, as well as the ingenuity of the accompaniment, and united force of the whole band, augmented throughout by the *tromboni*, when every voice and every instrument was employed, must have astonished, by the novelty of the effects, not only the unlearned lovers of Music, but the most scientific and experienced Musicians present.

FOURTH HAUTBOIS CONCERTO *(a)*.

I received such pleasure in my youth from all the six admirable Concertos, of which this is one, that as I had not heard them performed for many years, I rejoiced much to see two of them in the list of Commemoration-pieces; and still more, on hearing them, to find that they had not lost ground in my affection. To assert that they were never so well performed before, even under the author's own direction, is saying but little; as he was never master of so numerous or well disciplined a band. Indeed, such is the power of good performance, that it will give meaning and interest to ordinary Music; but compositions so intrinsically

(a) During the Opera regency of the Royal Academy, the Directors, at the close of a season, finding their finances in a better state than usual, determined to sacrifice a night to the emolument of the *Orchestra*. And a Concert being thought most likely to turn out profitable, Dr. Arbuthnot undertook to manage, and HANDEL to compose an Overture on the occasion. It was then that he produced this fourth Concerto, which from the use to which it was applied, was called the *Orchestra Overture*.

good

good as thefe, fo rich in harmony, melody, and contrivance, muft be ftill more heightened and fublimed. The opening of this fourth Hautbois Concerto is full, bold, and fpirited, in the Overture ftyle; the fecond movement is conftructed upon one of the moft airy themes, that ever was made the fubject of fugue; and it is ftill chequered, and enlivened by Mifcellaneous paffages. The third movement is a very agreeable Air, in minuet time, *alla caccia*. Indeed, this movement is fo much in the French-horn ftyle, that it feems to call for that inftrument. The fourth movement is a fhort fugue, in a minor key, with folo parts for the two violins. The *finale* is a very pleafing minuet, with a folo part for a baffoon. The late celebrated performer on that inftrument, Miller, ufed to acquire great applaufe by his tone, and manner of playing this movement, at public places. It was now performed by twenty-four baffoons, of which the unity of effect was truly marvellous. The violoncellos were very judicioufly ordered to play only the under part in this ftrain.

And here it feems but indifpenfable juftice to obferve, that Mr. Fifcher performed the folo parts of this Concerto, upon the Hautbois, with fuch exquifite tafte and propriety, as muft have convinced all thofe who heard him, that his excellence is not confined to the performance of his own very original and inge-nious productions. Indeed, one of the Commemoration-wonders feems to have been, the perfect manner with which the fweet and grateful tone of his fingle inftrument filled the ftupendous building, where this excellent Concerto was performed.

I have dwelt the longer on this Concerto as it is one of the moft mafterly and pleafing of HANDEL's inftrumental productions. It was the fafhion, during his life-time, to regard his compofitions for violins, as much inferior to thofe of Corelli and

P   Gemi-

Geminiani; but I think very unjuftly. If thofe two great maf-ters knew the finger-board and genius of their own inftrument better than HANDEL, it muft be allowed, *per contra*, that he had infinitely more fire and invention than either of them. Co-relli was naturally graceful, fymmetrical, and polifhed, but timid; Geminiani more bold, inventive, and rhapfodical, was frequently deficient in rhythm, and air. Indeed, his Mufic is fo little phrafed, that whenever a young performer, who plays a fubordi-nate part, is out, he can never get in again; whereas the me-lody of Corelli is fo meafured, that the number of bars, like feet in poetry, are even and correfpondent; fo that an inexpert player, with a tolerable ear, if thrown out, can have little difficulty in rallying.

These three admirable authors, who have fo long delight-ed Englifh ears, have certainly a diftinct character and ftyle of compofition, wholly diffimilar from each other: they would all, doubtlefs, have been greatly fublimed by the performance of fuch a band as that lately affembled; but HANDEL in a fuperior degree: as the bold defigns, maffes of harmony, contraft, and conftant refources of invention, with which his works abound, require a more powerful agency to develope and difplay them, than the mild ftrains of Corelli, or the wilder effufions of Geminiani.

HANDEL fports with a band, and turns it to innumer-able unexpected accounts, of which neither Corelli nor Gemi-niani had ever the leaft want or conception. He certainly ac-quired, by writing fo long for voices and an opera band, more experience and knowledge of effects than either of thefe ad-mirable violinifts: fo that fuppofing their genius to be equal, thefe circumftances muft turn the fcale in his favour. Indeed, HANDEL was always afpiring at *numbers* in his fcores and in his Orcheftra; and nothing can exprefs his grand conceptions, but

an

an omnipotent band: the generality of his productions in the hands of a few performers, is like the club of Alcides, or the bow of Ulyſſes, in the hands of a dwarf.

A N T H E M.

" *O ſing unto the Lord, a new ſong,*" &c.

Chorus.

" *The Lord ſhall reign for ever and ever,*" &c.

After the Anthem and Chorus, which were performed with the ſame preciſion, and heard with the ſame unremitting eager-neſs of attention, as before, at the firſt performance in the Abbey, the

C O R O N A T I O N A N T H E M;

" *Zadock the prieſt, and Nathan the prophet,*" &c.

Terminated the exquiſite performance of this day; which though augmented by the addition of two Concertos, and two Choruſes, was ſo far from appearing long, that there ſeemed not to be a ſingle hearer, who did not regret its concluſion. And it would be ungrateful not to confeſs, that all the additional pieces of this day's miſcellany were ſo judiciouſly choſen and admirably exe-cuted, as to reflect the higheſt honour upon the great Muſician, who not only gave occaſion to the Feſtival, but furniſhed food for the Feaſt.

COM-

Pl. VII.

View of the **ORCHESTRA** and Performers in Westminster Abbey during the Commemoration of **HANDEL**.

Published, January 14th 1785.

COMMEMORATION

OF

HANDEL.

FIFTH PERFORMANCE;

THE

MESSIAH.

By COMMAND OF HER MAJESTY,

In WESTMINSTER-ABBEY,

Saturday, June 5, 1784.

THOUGH this fublime production was performed here but a week before, in fo perfect and magnificent a manner, that no rehearfal, previous to its repetition, was neceffary to the band; yet, to gratify the wifhes of many timid and infirm lovers of Mufic, who dreaded the croud that was likely to be affembled at a public performance, as well as to raife money for charitable purpofes, another rehearfal would certainly have been announced for Friday, if it had not been prevented from taking place by the celebration of his Majefty's birth-day, on which occafion there was a certainty that the chief part of the performers and company would be engaged.

Thofe who attended this day's Commemoration at the Abbey were, feemingly, of a higher clafs than had yet appeared there; fo that though the croud was fomewhat lefs than at the preceding performance of the fame Oratorio, the exhibition was more fplendid. Indeed, as a fpectacle, it was fo magnificent to the fight, and, as a mufical performance, fo mellifluous and grateful to the ear, that it will be difficult for the *mind's eye* of thofe who were abfent, to form an adequate idea of the fhow, or the *mental ear* of the found, from defcription. Every one prefent muft have found full employment for the two fenfes which afford us the moft refined pleafure; as it is from the eye and the ear that intellect is fed, and the mind furnifhed with its beft intelligence.

There

There was a change in the manner of executing the Mufic to " *Lift up your heads, O ye gates*," which deferves to be mentioned. On the former occafion, the alternate femi-chorufes were performed by *all* the voices belonging to each part ; but to-day, in order to heighten the contraft, only by three of the principal fingers, till about the thirty-third bar ; when the whole Chorus from each fide of the Orcheftra, joined by all the inftruments, burft out, " *He is the king of glory*." This had a moft admirable effect, and brought tears into the eyes of feveral of the performers. Indeed, if we may judge from the plenitude of fatiffaction which appeared in the countenances of all prefent, this effect was not fuperficial, nor confined to the Orcheftra.

Another new and grand effect was produced to-day in the Hallelujah, and laft Chorus, " *Worthy is the Lamb*," by the introduction of the *tromboni*, which were not ufed in thefe Chorufes, on the former occafion.

At the firft performance of the Mefliah, his Majefty expreffed a defire to the earl of Sandwich of hearing the moft truly fublime of all Choruffes : " *Allelujah ! for the Lord God omnipotent reigneth*," a fecond time ; and this gracious wifh was conveyed to the Orcheftra, by the waving of his lordfhip's wand. At this fecond performance of that matchlefs Oratorio, his Majefty was pleafed to make the fignal himfelf, with a 'gentle motion of his right hand in which was the printed book of the words, not only for the repetition of this, but of the final Chorus, in the laft part, to the great gratification of all his happy fubjects prefent ; and, perhaps, the fubjects of no fovereign prince on the globe were ever before fo delighted with the effects of a royal mandate.

Thus ended the fifth and laft of the performances for this memorable celebration ; and fo great and perfect was the pleafure
which

which the audience had received, that those who had attended all the five exhibitions, seemed most to regret this final close. There remains, however, a hope, that a performance, somewhat similar, may be annually established under the auspices of their Majesties and the same Directors, for the Benefit of the MUSICAL FUND. The plan is not yet wholly digested; but I have authority to say that their Majesties have graciously condescended to take this Society and Charity under their Royal patronage and protection; that the noblemen and baronets who so admirably directed the late Commemoration, have deigned to become in a particular manner patrons of the institution, by accepting the offices of honorary President and Vice-Presidents of this Society; and that an annual performance, on a grand and extensive scale, is in meditation, at which pieces selected from the works of the immortal HANDEL, now consecrated by time, reason, science, and universal approbation, will be performed in the most perfect and splendid manner possible.

This information may, perhaps, a little abate the despair of those lovers of Music, who imagined that such an artificial want was created, by the late grand and exquisite performances, as it was impossible ever again to gratify: regarding the concurrence of favourable circumstances which produced such an audience, and such a performance, as totally out of the reach of purchase or power of chance.

Indeed the late performances, for some time, so diminished the effect of Orchestras which always used to be thought the most considerable, that many of the performers in the Opera-band, after having been at the Abbey on the two Saturday mornings of Commemoration, imagined, at night, that half their brethren were absent, and the other half, asleep.

Q   And

And though there may, perhaps, be a difference of opinion concerning the comparative excellence of particular movements in the compofitions of each day, as well as the performance of individuals ; yet the effects and perfection of the whole ; the precifion with which this mufical phalanx moved, and weight and dignity it gave to every feries of founds in melody, and combination in harmony, can only be controverted by extreme ignorance, or perfect infenfibility. But if, befides thefe, there fhould ftill be others, who, wifhing to be thought more delicate in their feelings, and accurate in their decifions than the reft of mankind, are unwilling to do juftice to thefe performances ; they may furely be afked what *is* good mufic, and good performance, if fuch as produced thefe effects be denied that title ? Let us, at leaft, have fome fuperior ftandard of excellence erected, under which to enlift, before we abandon fenfibility to the mercilefs feverity of unprincipled critics, who feem at war, not only with candour, truth, and good tafte, but with their own pleafures.

Being very defirous to know what judicious foreigners thought of thefe exhibitions, particularly Italians, accuftomed to good Mufic in their churches, as well as theatres, I applied to *Count Benincafa*, a Venetian nobleman, who was then in London, and had been prefent at the performance of the MESSIAH in Weftminfter-Abbey, for information concerning the comparative grandeur and excellence of this Band, with any other which he had heard, or of which hiftory or tradition had preferved the memory, in his own country. As we had not time for a full difcuffion of the fubject, when it was firft propofed, *viva voce, Signor Benincafa* was fo obliging as to honour me with his opinion in a letter, of which, before his departure, I entreated his permiffion to lay an extract before the public ; and it will be the

more

more flattering to the projectors and executors of this stupendous plan, as the Count is an excellent judge of Music; having heard, read, meditated, and written on the subject, with a degree of feeling and intelligence, that is equally honourable to himself and the art *(a)*.

London, June 7, 1784.

Dear Sir,

THE Commemoration of HANDEL, celebrated in London during the months of May and June 1784, is one of those events which every friend of humanity should reverence and exalt, for the honour of mankind. Happily for you, Sir, the friend of humanity in this sense, ought in a particular manner to be a friend to the English. It is only your great and very respectable nation that is capable of planning and executing such enterprizes as carry us back to heroic times, by their grandeur and sublimity.

De Londres ce 7 Juin, 1784.

Monsieur, et très-cher Ami,

LA Commémoration de HANDEL célébrée à Londres aux mois de Mai et Juin 1784, est un de ces événemens que tout ami des hommes doit remarquer, et exalter pour l'honneur de ses semblables. Heureusement pour vous, Monsieur, l'ami des hommes me paroit dans ce sens devoir être surtout l'ami des Anglois. C'est à vôtre grand et toute respectable nation, qu'il appartient d'imaginer, et d'exécuter les idées, qui peuvent nous retracer les tems héroïques par leur élévation, et par le sentiment exquis, et sublime à la fois, qu'elles déployent.

(a) See *Essai sur la Musique*, tom. iii. Par. 1780, 4to. where there are many articles concerning Italian composers and singers, with which *Count Benincasa* furnished the editor, that breathe the true spirit of taste, sensibility, and enthusiasm.

In

In the character of a true Italian, tormented by his fenfibility, unlefs he gives it vent aloud, I neither can be filent, nor fufficiently explain to you, how much I refpected the idea, and was ftruck with the majefty of its execution.

To honour in this manner the memory of an author, who has fignalized himfelf fo much in the divine art of Mufic, though a foreigner; an author who had the merit of breaking up new ground, and fowing it with the immortal feeds of knowledge and genius, which time, however, and the limits affigned by nature to our exiftence have not allowed him to fee grow up to their prefent degree of perfection, is an event the moft honourable to that nation which renders fuch public and difinterefted juftice to the fimple and filent merit of an illuftrious mortal, who is now no more. Why, alas! did not his fhade hover round his portrait, and enjoy the triumph *(a)*?

En qualité de bon Italien que fa fenfibilité tourmente, s'il ne la foulage pas en criant autour de lui, je ne puis ni me taire, ni vous dire affez, combien j'ai été touché de cet idée, et frappé de l'enfemble majeftueux de fon exécution.

Honorer de cette maniere la mémoire d'un auteur des plus fignalés dans le bel art divin de la Mufique, mais qui étoit etranger; d'un auteur, qui a eu le mérite de défricher un champ prefqu' inculte dans ce fol, en y fémant des germes immortels de favoir, et de génie, mais à qui le tems, et les bornes affignés par la nature à tout inventeur, quelqu' étonnant qu'il fut, n'ont pas permis de porter fon ouvrage à la perfection qu'on a plus aifément atteinte depuis; c'eft un des faftes les plus honorables pour la nation, qui rend une juftice fi éclatante, fi defintéreffée au mérite fimple et muet d'un mort illuftre. Pourquoi fon ombre, en voltigeant autour de fon portrait, n'a-t-elle pû jouir de ce beau triomphe?

(a) The portrait of HANDEL was placed in the front of the Orcheftra.

I fhall

I shall long have before my eyes that beautiful temple whose pointed vaults ascend to heaven; that immense croud of the most beautiful and wealthy inhabitants of the first city in the universe; the interesting spectacle of a Royal Family, whose beauty charms, and whose goodness captivates every eye and heart; and that prodigious Orcheftra, which never before had exiftence on the earth, and which by its admirable arrangement feemed like Mufic itfelf, to defcend from the fkies.

I have in vain tortured my memory to find any feftival fimilar to this, either in hiftory or fable. Perhaps, a noify croud of trumpets, bells, harps, and drums, ftunned the inhabitants of Babylon, when the good king Nabuchodonofor vifited them in all his Afiatic pomp; perhaps, the wife king Solomon, in his great abundance of every thing, made the vaults of the temple ring with his innumerable copper veffels, ruftic pipes, and brazen triangles.

J'aurai longtems devant mes yeux ce temple, qui pouffe au ciel fes voutes aigües, cette foule nombreufe, l'elite des beaux et riches habitans de la premiere ville de l'univers, l'afpect toujours intéreffant d'une Famille Royale, dont la beauté arrête tous les yeux, et la bonté captive tous les cœurs, cet Orcheftre immenfe, qui n'a jamais exifté auparavant fur la terre, et qui paroiffoit dans fon arrangement fi bien entendu defcendre des cieux, comme la Mufique qui en eft la fille.

J'ai beau tourmenter ma memoire : elle ne me rappelle rien de femblable dans tous les faftes de l'hiftoire, et de la fable. Peut-être une foule bruyante de trompettes, de tymbales, de guitarres étourdiffoit les places de Babylone, lorfque la bonne bête du roi Nabuchodonofor les traverfoit dans fa pompe Afiatique : peut-être le grand roi Salomon, qui avoit tout par milliers, faifoit-il rétentir les voutes du temple par le grand nombre de fes plats de cuivre, de fes fifres fauvages et de fes triangles d'airain.

But

But certainly, fince the inexhauftible riches and variety of harmony were firft difplayed, I believe that it has not been poffible, till now, to affemble upwards of five hundred Muficians, and which is ftill more extraordinary, without impeding by their number, the moft accurate and finifhed execution.

No one, Sir, is better acquainted with the Mufical Feftivals of Italy than yourfelf. But thofe of the greateft magnitude at the courts of Florence, Ferrara, Parma, or Naples, during the two laft centuries, offer nothing equal in number, to the fpectacle in Weftminfter-Abbey.

You have been pleafed to afk me whether the city of Venice, which has been celebrated at all times for the fplendor of its public reprefentations, has lately had any Mufical exhibition approaching in magnificence to the Commemoration of HANDEL.

Mais furement depuis que l'harmonie a déployé fes richeffes, fes variétés inépuifables, je crois qu'on n'a jamais ni pû, ni fû raffembler cinq cent ving cinq Muficiens, dont le nombre étonnant n'a pas nui à l'éxecution la plus jufte, la plus finie.

Perfonne ne connoit, comme vous, Monfieur, les faftes de la Mufique Italienne: les grandes fêtes des cours de Florence, de Ferrare, de Parme aux deux derniers fiecles, lors de la renaiffance de la Mufique, celles de Naples aux occafions des événemens de cour, ne vous ont préfenté, quant au nombre, rien de comparable au fpectacle de Weftminfter-Abbey.

Vous avez la bonté de me demander, fi la ville de Vénife, qui eft en poffeffion depuis tant de fiecle de donner des fpectacles auffi finguliers, qu'elle, et dont le département mufical eft des plus confidérables en Italie, n'a pas peut-être fourni dernierément quelqu'exemple d'une magnificence, qui approche de la Commémoration de HANDEL.

And

And I freely own to you that we can boaſt of nothing equally numerous. Indeed, I am perſuaded, that it requires near a million of inhabitants, and as great a paſſion for Muſic as there is at preſent in London, to furniſh upwards of five hundred profeſſional Muſicians. Conſequently, whatever genius the Italians may poſſeſs for Muſic, as we have no city ſo peopled, we can never aſſemble ſuch a number of muſical profeſſors, without collecting them from many ſtates and capitals (a).

The memory of the following events, however, is honourably preſerved by the Venetians. During the reſidence of their moſt ſerene highneſſes the Comte and Comteſſe du Nord, in Venice, 1782, the republic regaled them with ſeveral

Je vous réponds d'abord trés-décidement, que non, quant au nombre des Muſiciens. Je ſuis perſuadé qu'il ne faut rien moins que preſqu'un million d'habitans, et autant de luxe dans la Muſique qu'il y en a à Londres, pour mettre enſemble plus de cinq cent bons Muſiciens par état. Conſéquemment, quel que ſoit le talent des Italiens pour la Muſique, comme il eſt très-vrai, et très-naturel, qu'on la ſait en Italie mieux qu'ailleurs, cependant comme nous n'avons pas a beaucoup prés aucune ville de cette force ; il ne pourra jamais y avoir un aſſemblage pareil de profeſſeurs en Muſique, à moins qu'on ne les ramaſſe de pluſieurs villes.

Voici, pourtant, quelques événemens Vénitiens, dont on peut conſerver un ſouvenir honorable.

A l'occaſion du ſéjour que LL. AA. SS. le Comte et la Comteſſe du Nord firent à Véniſe en 1782, la Republique leur donna des

(a) Though upwards of five hundred Muſicians were employed in the performance of the *Meſſiah*, at the Commemoration of HANDEL, yet ſuch is the preſent muſical ſtrength of this country, that it could have furniſhed an equal number for the other end of the Abbey, had they been wanted, with Giardini, Barthelemon, Salomon, &c. at their head.

ſuperb

superb spectacles, of which a very exact and interesting description, interspersed with national anecdotes, has been published by an English lady, settled at Venice. Among other festivals they were presented with a *Cantata*, composed by Mortellari, a Neapolitan, and executed by a hundred Musicians, male and female. A Concert and a Ball were likewise made for the same illustrious strangers, at the theatre of Saint Benedict. The band of Musicians all dressed in a rich uniform, exceeded a hundred, and had a very good effect.

But the most singular event, was the entertainment given to the present Emperor on his first arrival in Italy; a festival as extraordinary of its kind as that of London. All the girls in the four Conservatorios, or Music-Schools, able to perform vocally or instrumentally, were collected. Signor Bertoni, maestro di Capella of one of these Conservatorios, composed a *Cantata* ex-

fêtes superbes, dont il y a une description fort exacte, et très-intéressante d'ailleurs par plusieurs détails nationaux, qui est l'ouvrage d'une dame Angloise établie à Vénise. Parmi ces fêtes on leur donna une Cantate composée par le sieur Mortellari, Napolitain, maître de Musique dans cette ville, et exécutée par une centaine de Musiciens, et Musiciennes. Une autre soirée fut employée à leur donner dans le grand théatre de St. Benoît, un Concert, et un Bal. La bande des Musiciens, tous habillés en uniforme riche, passoit la centaine, et la fête eut un très-bel effet.

Mais l'événement le plus singulier, car je le crois tout aussi unique dans ses circonstances, que celui de Londres pour le nombre, est la fête que l'on donna à S. M. L'Empereur à son premier voyage en Italie.

On tira des quatre Conservatoires, ou hôpitaux fameux, toutes les filles en état de rendre quelque partie vocale, ou instrumentale. Le Sieur Bertoni, maître Venitien très-connu, composa à cette oc-

pressly

preſſly on the occaſion; and in the immenſe hall of the *Rezzo-nico* palace a band was collected, conſiſting of one hundred and twenty girls, uniformly, modeſtly, and elegantly dreſſed. Every kind of inſtrument, and every ſpecies of voice, including double-baſes, wind-inſtruments, vocal *tenors*, and *baſes*, were ſupplied by young female hands, and female throats. And there was no other man among them than the compoſer, who was a ſilent and inactive auditor. It is true, that the number of theſe fell very ſhort of five hundred; but will not the ſingularity and the diffi-culty of forming ſuch an aſſembly of Sirens augment their value and importance? Twenty pieces of gold may be of infinitely more value than a hundred of ſilver; and, in the preſent caſe, there is, perhaps, the metallic difference which renders the two ſums equal. And you will not, I hope, Sir, deny that one hun-dred girls may be a match for five hundred men, in Muſic. And

caſion une cantate exprés, et l'on vit dans la ſalle immenſe du palais Rezzonico *un Orcheſtra de cent vingt filles en uniforme modeſte et gentil: toute ſorte d'inſtrumens, tout rôle de chant, y compris la contre-baſſe, et les inſtrumens à vent, les* tenori, *et les* baſſes-tailles *pour le chant, tout etoit deſſervi par des jeunes mains, et des jeunes goziers de filles: et il n'y avoit d'autre homme au milieu d'elles, que le maître compoſiteur, qui ne faiſoit qu'aſſiſter.—Il eſt vrai qu'il y a encore bien loin de ce nombre à cinq cent; mais auſſi combien la proportion, qui réſulte de la ſingularité, et de la difficulté d'unir tant de jeunes perſonnes du ſex n'augmente t-il pas la valeur de ce nombre? Vingt pieces d'or peuvent en valoir plus de cent en argent: et dans nôtre cas il y a une différence de métal, pour ainſi dire, qui rend peut-être les deux ſommes égales. Entre nous, avouez d'ailleurs, Monſieur, que cent filles peuvent bien tenir tête a cinq cent hommes, en Muſique.*

R   pray

pray remember that they were very well in tune; which is the more remarkable, confidering their vivacity, quarrels, little acquaintance with each other, inexperience, and the ufual jealoufy of rival fchools. Obferve, likewife, that fuch an Orcheftra as this, independent of its Mufical merit, is very interefting, and that the charms of fex is equal to the moft powerful effects.

This is all, my dear friend, that my memory can furnifh at prefent, in anfwer to your queftions; but as I am far from thofe fcenes of action, and as you have not allowed me time to procure better information, by letter, I will not anfwer for the precifion of my narrative.

Notez, qu'elles allerent fort bien d'accord, ce qui eft encore plus rémarquable, vû leur vivacité, leur inexpérience de fe trouver enfemble, et les petites tracafferies qui tiennent à leur état, et à la jaloufie réciproque des endroits d'où elles fortoient. Avouez de même, qu'un Orcheftre pareil, independamment de fon mérite Mufical, eft très intéreffant, et que ce même mérite ainfi placé, a tout le droit au plus grands effets.

Voilà, Monfieur et très cher ami, ce que ma mémoire m'a fourni fur le champ, pour pouvoir répondre immediatement à vos queftions. Mais comme je fuis loin des lieux, et que vous n'avez pas voulu me donner le tems de me faire écrire ces chofes plus en détail, je ne réponds pas de la derniere exactitude dans les circonftances que j'ai rapportées.

I feize

I feize, however, with the greateft eagernefs this opportunity of teftifying my regard, and of affuring you that

I have the honour to be, Sir,

Your moft humble and moft obedient

Servant and Friend,

LE COMTE BENINCASA.

J'ai faifi avec le plus grand plaifir l'occafion de vous témoigner, quoique fi imparfaitement, ma confideration pour vôtre mérite perfonnel, mon eftime pour la juftesse et l'etendue de vos lumieres, et, permettez-moi de dire auffi, ma reconnoissance pour vôtre zele éclairé, qui a repandu tant de jour et de philofophie fur l'hiftoire de la Mufique, de cette fource intariffable de plaifir, et de fentiment, que la Divinité bienfaifante a ouverte aux mortels.

J'ai l'honneur d'être, Monfieur,

Votre très-humble et très-obeiffant

Serviteur, et Ami,

LE COMTE BENINCASA.

STATE of MONEY received, in confequence of the Five Commemoration Mufical Performances.

	£.	s.	d.
Received the firft day, at Weftminfter-Abbey, Wednefday, May 26, 1784 -	2966	5	0
Second Performance, in the Pantheon, Thurf-day, May 27 - -	1690	10	0
Third Performance, in the Abbey, Saturday, May 29 - -	2626	1	0
Fourth Performance—Thurfday, June 3 -	1603	7	0
Fifth Performance—Saturday, June 5 -	2117	17	0
At three feveral Rehearfals, in Weftminfter-Abbey and Pantheon - -	944	17	10
His Majefty's moft gracious donation -	525	0	0
By fale of printed books of the words -	262	15	0
Whole Receipts - - - - £.	12736	12	10

Dif-

Difburfement of SUMS expended, and appropriated to Charitable Purpofes.

	£.	s.	d.
To Mr. James Wyatt, for building, in the Abbey and the Pantheon	1969	12	0
Mr. Afhley for payment of the band, &c.	1976	17	0
Rent and illumination of the Pantheon	156	16	0
Advertifing in Town and Country Papers	236	19	0
Printing books of the words	289	2	0
Door-keepers	102	1	6
Ufe of the organ	100	0	0
High, and petty conftables	100	5	0
Gratifications	167	5	0
Engraving cheques and tickets, ftriking medals, drawings, guards, porters, and fundry incidents	351	8	10
To the Society for decayed Muficians	6000	0	0
To the Weftminfter Hofpital	1000	0	0
In the hands of Redmond Simpfon, Sub-treafurer, to anfwer fubfequent demands	286	6	6
Whole Difburfement, errors excepted £.	12736	12	10

REDMOND SIMPSON (a).

(a) Sir Watkin Williams Wynn, who involved and embarraffed himfelf with the troublefome and complicated office of *Treafurer*, undertaking, *ex Officio*, to receive and difburfe fums of money fufficient to have employed the clerks of a confiderable banker's-fhop, had great affiftance from the zeal, diligence, and arithmetic-dexterity of Mr. Simpfon, a veteran profeffor, no lefs diftinguifhed for his abilities and probity, than active in all that tends to the profperity of the Fund, and honour of his profeffion.

APPEN-

APPENDIX.

A P P E N D I X.

THE fums raifed in fo fhort a fpace of time by the productions of one Compofer only, fo long after his deceafe, and that of almoft all his perfonal friends and acquaintance, whofe partiality could be fuppofed to operate on the occafion, may be numbered among the *miraculous powers* of modern Mufic.

And as the great fhare of the profits arifing from the Commemoration-performances which have been beftowed on the FUND *for the Support of Decayed Muficians and their Families*, may excite curiofity concerning the nature, extent, and utility, of that inftitution, and its claim to fo confiderable a bounty, I fhall here give an extract from the original ftatutes of the Society, followed by a few reflections on its fubfequent profperity and ufe.

ABSTRACT of the LAWS and RESOLUTIONS of the FUND *for the Support of Decayed Muficians and their Families.*

May 8, 1738.

" WHEREAS a Subfcription was fet on foot the beginning of the laft month, for eftablifhing a FUND *for the Support of Decayed Muficians, or their Families*; which Subfcription having already met with uncommon fuccefs, the Subfcribers have had two General Meetings, in order to form themfelves into a regular

S   Society

Society, by the name of THE SOCIETY OF MUSICIANS, and have elected Twelve Governors for the prefent year ; and alfo agreed to the following refolutions.

I. " That every fubfcriber to this Charity do pay, at leaft, Half a Crown a Quarter ; the firft payment to be made on or before Midfummer-day next *(a)*.

II. " That there be annually, on the Sunday before Midfummer-day, a general meeting of the faid Subfcribers, to infpect the accounts, and to elect Twelve Governors by ballot ; and that the faid Governors, or any five of them, fhall have power of receiving all monies collected for this charity, paying the fame as foon as poffible into the hands of Mr. *Andrew Drummond*, banker, upon account, and for the ufe of this SOCIETY ; there to remain until it arife to a fum capable of being put out at intereft in fome fund fecured by parliament.

III. " That the faid Governors, or any five of them, fhall have power of drawing upon Mr. *Andrew Drummond*, for fuch fums as fhall be wanted for the ufe of this Charity, and (under fuch reftrictions as fhall be judged neceffary by the SOCIETY) to difpofe of the fame, keeping an exact account, ready to be produced to any Subfcriber when defired.

IV. " That no perfon, or his family, fhall receive any benefit from this FUND, who has not been a profeffor of Mufic, and alfo a Subfcriber to this Charity, at leaft one year ; and that fuch perfon fhall produce a certificate, figned by ten Subfcribers, who are not Governors, of his being a proper object, before he fhall be entitled to any relief from the faid FUND.

(*a*) In 1766, the fum of twenty fhillings per annum was required of all new-elected members, inftead of ten.   And the old members then agreed, almoft unanimoufly, to pay the fame fum.

5. " That

V. " That no man who has not a family, fhall receive of this FUND more than Ten Shillings-a week, except in cafe of ficknefs, an allowance for advice and medicines, at the difcretion of the Governors for the time being.

VI. " That a weekly allowance, not exceeding Seven Shillings, be made to the widows of fuch Muficians (who have been Subfcribers to this Fund) as are really found to be in want; but the faid allowance *to ceafe if they marry again.*

VII. " That care fhall be taken of the children of fuch Muficians (who have been Subfcribers to this FUND) as are left deftitute of other fupport.

VIII. " That an allowance, not exceeding Five Pounds, be made for the funeral of every fuch Mufician (who has been a Subfcriber to this FUND) as fhall die without leaving effects fufficient to defray the expences of a decent interment, conditionally, that fuch perfon continued a Subfcriber to this Charity until the time of his death.

IX. " That in order to make a regular diftribution of this Charity, there be a meeting of the Governors the firft Sunday in every month, at the Cardigan-head Tavern, near Charing-crofs, or any other place that fhall be agreed upon by the Governors for the time being; at which meetings the Governors fhall have a power of admitting fuch perfons to fubfcribe to this FUND, as they fhall judge *not likely* to become foon a charge to it; and that no perfon be admitted a Subfcriber, but fuch as fhall be approved of by the faid Governors, or a majority of them.

X. " That no allowance whatever be made to the Governors for their faid Monthly meetings, but that all fuch meetings be at their own expence.

XI. " That

XI. " That all such Subscribers as are professors of Music, shall pay their subscriptions, or cause them to be paid, into the hands of the Governors, at some of the said Monthly meetings; and that a person be appointed (with a salary of Five Pounds a a year) *(a)* to collect the subscriptions of those persons who are not professors of Music.

XII. " That if any Subscriber neglect to pay his subscription for three quarters, he and his family shall be for ever excluded any benefit arising from this FUND.

XIII. " That the Governors shall be obliged to call a General Meeting of the Society, whenever it is required by any Twenty of the Subscribers.

XIV. " That in cases not provided for by the aforesaid Articles, the Governors, for the time being, shall have power of acting by such resolutions of their own making, as from time to time shall become necessary; but shall be obliged to report all such resolutions to the next General Meeting, in order to have them confirmed *(b)*".

In 1739, a compact was formed with the Corporation of *the Sons of the Clergy*, by which the SOCIETY engaged to furnish a band, selected from their subscribing members, for the two annual performances in St. Paul's Cathedral, in consideration of the sum of Fifty pounds, which the Corporation agreed to allow each year to the SOCIETY; and this sum has been constantly thrown into the FUND, and appropriated to charitable purposes.

(a) The Collector's salary in 1751, was augmented to 25 *l.* per annum.

(b) As the most rigid œconomy was absolutely necessary during the infancy of the Society, these fundamental laws, however, illiberal and contracted they may at present appear, were, perhaps, the best which could then be allowed or devised; but now the capital of the FUND is become so considerable, and expectations from future plans so promising, they certainly require immediate revisal and extension.

Besides

Befides the cafual and fluctuating income arifing from Subfcriptions and Benefits, the SOCIETY has been honoured with a few benefactions in the way of *Legacies*, of which the following is an account.

	£.	s.	d.
In 1758, Mr. *Claudio Rojere*, a profeffional Subfcriber to the FUND, bequeathed to its ufe the fum of	100	0	0
1760, Mr. *Boys Waldron*, ditto - - -	50	0	0
1782, Mr. *James Mathias*, merchant an honorary Subfcriber *(a)* - - -	50	0	0
But the moft confiderable bequeft which the Society has ever received from individual benevolence has been from its great benefactor, GEORGE FREDERIC HANDEL, who left to it the fum of -	1000	0	0

Concerning which Legacy the following account has been procured from the Minutes of the Society.

" *June* 17, 1759.

" Dr. *Bufwell*, late Gentleman of the Chapel-Royal, and one of the committee of the SOCIETY's accounts, reported, that Twelve Hundred and Fifty-four pounds ftock, of the reduced Bank Annuities, now ftanding in the names of Mr. *Thomas Wood*, Mr. *Peter Gillier*, and Mr. *Chriftian Reich*, in the books of the company of the Bank of England, had been transferred to them by *George Amyand*, efq. one of the exe-

---

(a) This worthy *Dilettante*, who was a conftant benefactor to the FUND from the time of its inftitution to his death, exclufive of his annual fubfcription, as an honorary member, frequently made prefents to the Charity, in money, at the time of the Benefit.

The admirably full, mellow, and extenfive bafe-voice of Mr. James Mathias will be long deplored by his friends, but particularly the members and frequenters of the *Crown and Anchor* Concert, who were fo long and fo highly delighted by its effects.

cutors

cutors of the laft Will and Teftament of GEORGE FREDERIC HANDEL, efq. deceafed, in full fatisfaction and difcharge of the Legacy of One Thoufand Pounds, given and bequeathed by the faid GEORGE FREDERIC HANDEL, in and by one of the Codicils to his laft Will, to the SOCIETY, by the name of *The* SOCIETY *for the Support of Decayed Muficians and their Families*; to be difpofed of in the moft beneficial manner for the fupport of that Charity."

By thefe donations; by the quarterly contributions of the Members of the SOCIETY during the firft years of the inftitution, and afterwards, when double that fum was required, by their annual payments; by honorary Subfcribers; and by Benefits, from June the 17th, 1739, to June the 20th, 1784, exclufive of the Six Thoufand Pounds from the Directors of the COMMEMORATION OF HANDEL, it appears, that in the courfe of forty-five years, the SOCIETY has not only accumulated a fum fufficient for the purchafe of £12,000, in South-fea Annuities and three *per Cents*, but has paid to their infirm and indigent brethren and their families £24,814 14s. ¾.

And it does appear that thefe fums have been diftributed in the moft upright and intelligent manner: allowing to each claiming Member

	£.	s.	d.
For his fubfiftence, per month – –	2	2	0
For a widow – – – –	1	10	4
For each child, the father being dead –	0	10	0
For fchooling, from five years old to eight, per quarter	0	10	0
From eight to fourteen – – –	0	15	0
For the funeral of a deceafed penfioner –	5	0	0

The

The SOCIETY, ever since its first institution, has not only been well supported by its principal Members, but by the public in general : for it appears, that the lowest annual sum received in the course of so many years, by Subscriptions and Benefit, has exceeded £400, except in 1766, when it only amounted to £134; and the highest sum, as in 1782 and 1783, has exceeded £1100.

Of these sums the money annually expended, except the two or three first years of the institution, has been from £120, to £866, which was disbursed in 1769.

	£.	s.	d.	
The SOCIETY's present pensioners are seven infirm and decayed brethren, at	2	2	0	each, per month.
Twenty-eight widows, at –	1	10	4	
Eleven children, at – –	0	10	0	

Other widows and children at different allowances proportioned to their situation and necessities; for the whole of which, with an allowance for the schooling of children of different ages, the SOCIETY at present, is at a certain current expence of –   –   £. 65 16 8 per month.

Or, –   –   –   790 0 0 per annum.

At their annual Benefits the principal professional Subscribers to the Charity, who are not employed in the Orchestra, are appointed to attend at the several doors and offices of the Theatre; the whole business being transacted by themselves, as regulated and ordered by a *Committee for the* CONCERT. And it seems as if no charitable institution could be more out of the reach of abuse, embezzlement, or partiality; regulated with more care, integrity, and œconomy; or have its income so immediately derived from

the

the activity and talents of its own Members. Except a small salary to the Secretary, and another to the Collector, there is no lucrative employment belonging to the institution: so that the whole produce of Benefits and Subscriptions is nett, and clear of all deduction or drawback.

Mr. *Michael Christian Festing*, and Doctor *Morrice Green*, took the lead at the time of instituting this Society, and for twelve or fourteen years afterwards. Since their decease, other Musicians, who were high in the profession, and of whose probity and honour their brethren had a good opinion, were placed, alternately, in the chair; and now, by the great accession to the Fund from the profits of the late Commemoration, its capital becomes a serious and weighty concern, amounting to upwards of £22,000, in South Sea annuities and three per Cents, which realizes, and ascertains, an income of £678 a year, exclusive of Benefit or Subscriptions.

The path therefore which the Governors and Court of Assistants have now to pursue is perfectly plain and pleasant: the power of alleviating distress and misery, of feeding the hungry, clothing the naked, and administering comfort to age and infirmities, is placed in their hands, without the trouble of providing the means.

* * * *

SOME

SOME illiberal reflexions having had admiffion into the Newf-papers, concerning the fmall gratuities that were accepted by in-dividuals in the *Commemoration-band*, as compenfations for a fort-night or three weeks labour and attendance, this feems the place for clearing them of the charge of meannefs or rapacity, by an exact ftatement of their fituation and fervices.

Indeed, it is natural for the Benefactors and friends of other Charities to look with an unfavourable eye upon the feeming partiality to the MUSICAL FUND, at the exclufion of all other inftitutions which have charity for their bafis. But a little in-formation concerning the peculiar claims of this SOCIETY, will, perhaps fatisfy the reafonable, if not filence the clamorous part of the public, who may intereft themfelves in the difpofal of the profits arifing from an enterprize, wholly generated and foftere by MUSIC.

And it may be neceffary to remind fuch perfons, that the firft object which occurred to the projectors of this Feftival, was not the raifing large fums of money; but the honour of the Mufical art, and of a great and favourite profeffor. And happy would they have been, during the firft dawnings of hope that fuch an idea could ever be realized, had any one to whom it it was commu-nicated been able to affure them, that the plan would *fupport itfelf*. When profeffional men, and particularly the Members of the MUSICAL FUND, were found willing to afford it all the fupport in their power, and there feemed a poffibility that the expences, great as they muft appear, in every point of view, would not only be defrayed by the performances in contemplation, but that there might, perhaps, be fome furplus to difpofe of, nothing could be more natural and reafonable than for the patrons of this

T   enter-

enterprize to fortify zeal in the performers, by the hope of be-coming benefactors to their own well-inftituted FUND.

But when it is remembered that public curiofity was ftimulated during the progrefs of the undertaking, in proportion to the fpontaneous ardor with which Muficians of all ranks gratuitoufly offered their affiftance, while it was fuppofed that the whole ce-lebrity would be comprifed in *two performances* on one and the *fame day*; that MUSIC was the origin, MUSIC the efficient and final caufe of the Feftival; and that the profeffors of no other fcience, art, or faculty, however fuperior in rank or utility, could, perhaps, fo effectually have influenced the public to fup-port at fo uncommon an expence, any other fpecies of exhi-bition: it can hardly be pronounced unreafonable that Muficians fhould form a wifh, and their patrons be willing to gratify fuch a wifh, that a charitable inftitution, founded folely for the fup-port of their aged, infirm, and indigent brethren, as well as wives, widows, children, and orphans, involved in their diftrefs, fhould be chiefly benefited by the fuccefs of this memorable celebration.

And with refpect to the fituation of Muficians in general, who bore a part in this COMMEMORATION, it may with the utmoft truth be afferted, that no eminent profeffor could either perform, or attend the performances, without facrificing very confiderably to the honour of HANDEL, and profperity of the SOCIETY. Even thofe that were paid received no compenfation that could be deemed at all adequate to the neglect of fcholars and other concerns, fo many days, in order to attend public and private re-hearfals, as well as the performances themfelves. Indeed, thofe profeffors, who paid for admiffion at all the five public exhibi-tions,

tions, of whom there were great numbers, fuftained the *leaft* damage. But even to them, five guineas, and the lofs confequent to four entire days abfence from bufinefs, at fuch a time of the year, muft have occafioned a confiderable difference in their affairs.

The worthy noblemen and baronets, who honoured the undertaking with their countenance and direction, wifely and generoufly hung out honourable lures of wands, good cheer, medals, and importance, to thofe who, without performing, were willing to take an active part in the bufinefs; yet it is but juftice to fay, that the honour of HANDEL and benefit of their favourite SOCIETY, ftimulated their zeal more powerfully than any other confiderations. And the total difintereftednefs and humanity with which the heads of the Mufical profeffion have acted for the welfare of this inftitution, their folicitude, and their pride, ever fince its firft eftablifhment, is the more honourable, as, befides their quarterly contributions, attendance at general and monthly Meetings as Governors, and fpending their own money at them all; the performing gratis at the annual benefit for the Charity, as well as thofe of the Sons of the Clergy, for the profit of the SOCIETY, are facrifices which no other profeffional men can boaft, merely for the maintenance and fupport of their infirm and unfortunate brethren and their families: as, by this means, they transfer the weight of providing for their neceffities, from the fhoulders of the public, to their own.

St. Martin's-ftreet,
July 1784.

E R R A T A.

PREFACE, Page xiii. *dele* line 2. *and infert* as if it had been produced by a few felect performers, in &c.

LIFE OF HANDEL, P. 13. l. 5. from the bottom, *dele* was. P. 24, Note *(a)*. l. 4. *read* Belchier. Ibid. Note *(b)*, *read* Sheridan. P. 28. l. 12, *dele* that. P. 38. l. 22, *for* were, *read* had. P. 46. *for* 2 vols. *read* a volume. P. 52. l. 10, *for* qui, *read* que.

COMMEMORATION. *Introduction.* P. 11. l. 18, *read* Dupuis. P. 12. Note *(a)* and elfewhere, *read* Afhley. P. 36. l. 13. *dele* s *in the word* fimples. P. 40, *dele the catchword* Indeed, *and infert* Nothing.

DIRECTIONS to the BINDER for placing the CANCELS.

Signature *B to be placed between B and C.

D 2 (a Sheet) and *D (a Quarter-Sheet) to be placed in Sheet D, inftead of Pages 19, 20, 21, and 22.

F p. 39 and 40 (laft Leaf) to be cancelled, and Sheet G follows immediately.

I a Quarter Sheet follows H.

Laft Leaf of *E* and firft of *F*, cancelled; to be replaced by the Half-Sheet marked *E and *F*.

See Directions for placing the PLATES, Firft Sheet, p. viii.